ning a
town around

Turning a
town around

a proactive approach to urban design

Tony Hall

Emeritus Professor of Town Planning, Anglia Ruskin University
Adjunct Professor, Griffith University, Brisbane

Blackwell
Publishing

© 2007 by Tony Hall

Blackwell Publishing editorial offices:
Blackwell Publishing Ltd, 9600 Garsington Road, Oxford OX4 2DQ, UK
    Tel: +44 (0)1865 776868
Blackwell Publishing Inc., 350 Main Street, Malden, MA 02148-5020, USA
    Tel: +1 781 388 8250
Blackwell Publishing Asia Pty Ltd, 550 Swanston Street, Carlton, Victoria 3053, Australia
    Tel: +61 (0)3 8359 1011

First published 2007 by Blackwell Publishing Ltd

ISBN-13: 978-1-4051-7023-9

Library of Congress Cataloging-in-Publication Data

Hall, A. C.
Turning a town around : a pro-active approach to urban design / Tony Hall.
    p. cm.
Includes bibliographical references and index.
   ISBN-13: 978-1-4051-7023-9 (pbk. : alk. paper)
   1. City planning. 2. Municipal engineering. I. Title.
TD160.H35 2007
307.1'216–dc22

                              2007012911

A catalogue record for this title is available from the British Library

Set in 10/12.5 Avenir
by Newgen Imaging Systems Pvt Ltd, Chennai, India
Printed and bound in Singapore
by Markono Print Media Pte Ltd

For further information on Blackwell Publishing, visit our website:
www.blackwellpublishing.com/construction

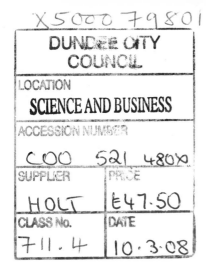
Table of contents

The colour plate section can be found between pages 104 and 105

Preface and acknowledgments

This book arises from my personal experience as a member of Chelmsford Borough Council, in particular during the period between 1996 and 2003. It has been written in a positive manner so that others may benefit from it. If readers have had similar experiences, as I would imagine to be the case, then I would urge them to do the same. The more that good practice is written down and published, the more will be the benefit. It is not difficult to understand why this does not happen more often. Practitioners undertaking good work and achieving results on the ground may often be under too much pressure to write accounts of what they are doing. Nevertheless, this omission is to the disadvantage of other practitioners and those studying to become practitioners, who may have to reinvent procedures or spend much time tracking down relevant information.

Whereas the process of writing the book has been my own work, its content reflects a team effort. By the end of the time period it covers, the team had become very large indeed. It went way beyond my fellow senior councillors, the responsible chief officers and the urban design team at Chelmsford. It embraced members of the Development Control and Development Plan sections of Planning Services, other officers and support staff and several members of Engineering Services. This team effort required the participation of many other councillors and officers who had a wide range of other responsibilities. By the end of the time period covered here, individual developers, and their planners and architects, were also playing positive and important roles. All were contributing to the progress made on the ground. Unfortunately, the very extent and complexity of the enterprise made it very difficult to make proper acknowledgment within the confines of this book. If one person was mentioned, then why not another? The list could have gone on for an almost endless number of pages. Another difficulty was that of distinguishing between different degrees of participation. They were finely graded over a wide range. Almost inevitably, this problem has meant that I have not been able to list everyone involved and I will have to trust that no one will be offended by the omission.

The names that must be mentioned, however, are those members of the urban design team whose work is reproduced within these pages. They are

Roy Chandler, Roger Estop and Dean Harris, who were employed by the Borough Council from 1990 to 2005, 1998 to date and 2002 to date, respectively. They deserve full credit for the quality of work shown. This includes the ways of proceeding recounted in this book as well as the published documents. In particular, the sections on a proactive approach and design principles in the Introduction, pages 11–12, a change of attitude in Chapter 1, page 21, and most of the content of Chapter 4 are drawn directly form the work of Roger Estop as prepared by him for dissemination in external presentations and seminars.

Notwithstanding the points made in the previous paragraph, I must also mention the names of my fellow councillor Andy Johnston, who was involved with implementing many of the changes described from the very beginning, and, above all, Stephen Ireland, who, first as corporate director and then deputy chief executive, ensured that what needed to happen did happen.

I am indebted to Chelmsford Borough Council for its permission to reproduce extracts from its planning documents and collection of photographs. I am also grateful to all of the architects, photographers and property developers whose work has been reproduced in the book. Their names are listed where appropriate in the table of sources of figures or are referred to in the text.

Tony Hall
Brisbane, Australia
February 2007

Abbreviations

CABE	Commission for Architecture and the Built Environment
CBC	Chelmsford Borough Council
ECC	Essex County Council
EPOA	Essex Planning Officers' Association
DETR	Department of the Environment, Transport and the Regions
DoE	Department of the Environment
DTLR	Department for Transport, Local Government and the Regions
DTp	Department of Transport
HMSO	Her Majesty's Stationary office
MfE	Ministry for the Environment, New Zealand
MoT	Ministry of Transport
PC	Parish Council
TCPA	Town and Country Planning Association
UTF	Urban Task Force

Introduction and context

A desire for a high standard of urban design has been manifest in many parts of the world for at least the last 20 years. The pursuit of safer and more sociable urban areas and more sustainable urban form has, fortunately, resulted in a considerable convergence of views on what outcomes are desirable. There is now an abundance of books and guides setting this out. In countries as far apart as Britain, as described herein, and New Zealand (MfE, 2005), governments have produced comprehensive policy statements in support of better design. What is less clear, however, is how a local planning agency makes a start in this direction and then manages to maintain high standards in the long term. This is not so much a matter of the goals but as how to go about it. If you are sitting at a desk in a local planning authority, what do you do to change things? What do you do if you work for a consultancy contracted to a local council? The responses to these questions involve more than what might be thought. It is these answers that this book tries to provide.

This book does not seek to provide these answers by promulgating general statements or idealised prescriptions, nor does it dwell on shortcomings and mistakes. It would have been easy to fill many pages with a critique of current practice and, in particular, of *reactive* responses to poor design. This approach has been eschewed in favour of a more positive line. What is set out is a practical programme of action based on direct experience.

Throughout the world, it is possible to encounter many good examples of achievement in urban design. In each place there will be story to be told. This book is based on the experience of one of them. In 2002, the British government invited local councils to enter a process that would select those with outstanding achievement in urban design for the accolade of Beacon Status for the Quality of the Built Environment. The successful ones were Cambridge, West Dorset and Chelmsford. All three will have their own story to recount. This is Chelmsford's. It is one in which the author was directly involved. It is set out here so that others may also benefit. Compared with other towns, Chelmsford was not especially favoured in terms of its built heritage or administrative record, and consequently there is no particular reason why its experience could not be replicated elsewhere. What was notable about its practice was, first, how both the spatial policy and detailed guidance expressed and prescribed the desired physical form and, second, how this was pursued through active negotiation (Hall and Estop, 2004). It was, above all, a *proactive approach*, and one that evolved though direct experience. It has been an approach that has delivered a high-quality urban environment and done so in a uniform manner, not merely through isolated examples. In the period 1996–2003 not just the policies but the life and appearance of the town were turned around.

Challenge and response

The problem of standardised housing

In many countries, the quality of design and layout for dwellings built for private sale has been problematic since at least the 1960s. It was certainly the case in Britain. In some parts of the country, it is a challenge that continues to the present day. By the early 1990s, most new estates of houses tended to look the same all over the country. The way they failed to contain space properly resulted in poor aesthetics and did not make the most economic use of land. They were also functionally suboptimal in terms of security, storage space and private amenity space such as back gardens. It was not always easy to find your way through the layouts or to serve them efficiently by public transport. This had not arisen by accident, or negligence, but for important reasons of process. In the absence of design intervention by planning authorities, the economics of house building in a situation of limited land supply produced a standard product.

The private purchaser does not, unfortunately, have much opportunity for exercising choice. In Britain, most people are not able to buy a plot of land and commission an architect and builder to create and build a house especially for them. Demand for dwellings exceeds supply, and for most people speculatively built housing developments are the only source of new dwellings. If house types are very similar, people buying new property have little choice of design. Furthermore, most purchasers do not possess the professional skills to make judgements on design in advance of living in a property. When owners later resell, they do not draw attention to the shortcomings of their property that they may have discovered through experience.

The supply of land for house building is regulated by the planning system, and the limited supply favours large companies who have the ability to purchase land in advance for high prices, in competition with each other. The house builders are not, however, the principal financial beneficiaries of the market. The people who make most money are the landowners with the prospect of planning permission. Neither the landowner nor developer has a long-term interest in the land, which will eventually all be sold on to individual purchasers or social landlords.

Having paid a large sum for the land, the house builder needs to recoup the investment as efficiently as possible. The incentive for the builder is to minimise costs while maximising selling price. Costs can be reduced by standardising dwelling types for mass production, going for cheaply built structures with add-on features. Decoration needs to be applied to the front only, where it is most conspicuous. With regard to selling price, customers acting as individuals do not have much economic leverage. House prices generally reflect supply and demand and the availability of credit. The price people are prepared to pay is governed by their ability to raise a mortgage in relation to their incomes. Whether the price is appropriate to the dwelling is checked by the lender with a local estate agent. Establishing the price for a dwelling is more a matter for financiers and estate agents rather than purchasers, and the process possesses a degree of circularity. In most countries, it is based on the gross floor area of the dwelling. Rather peculiarly, in Britain it reflects the number of bedrooms and whether or not the dwelling is detached. This process produces a distortion in the standard house-type. The incentive is to maximise the number of bedrooms for the minimum footprint of the dwelling. This is normally at the expense of the floor area devoted to reception rooms and storage space. 'Detached' can mean a separation of only 1.5 m, and in extreme cases, it may not be possible to pass between the dwellings. The result is a narrow range of standard types with very simple, low-cost roof shapes and a narrow gap between the dwellings.

The next stage in the process is to fit the dwellings to a particular site. Usually, this is done by a firm of architects or other designers who submit tenders for the work, the cheapest having the advantage. It is common for the roads to be drawn in first, making it difficult to fit the houses in afterwards. Standards for road widths and curves are laid down by the local highway authority. If, within the layout, standard dimensions are applied irrespective of the amount of pedestrian or vehicular traffic, then the space in front of the dwelling becomes wide in proportion to the height of the dwellings, resulting in a of loss of containment of space. Parking in front of the houses results in a townscape dominated by cars. The gross density and, consequently, the economics of the layout are also reduced.

As the dwellings have not been designed for the particular site, fitting them in becomes a challenge. This is made all the more difficult in the absence of corner and other types of dwelling that facilitate an effective overall composition. One result is the exposure of blank ends of buildings and the backs and sides of properties. This is not only an aesthetic problem but it also reduces the security of dwellings. Fitting the maximum number of dwellings along a given street encourages deep-plan forms that are difficult to light and ventilate naturally. Their narrow frontage also results in long, thin gardens, and the temptation then is to shorten them, resulting in very small back gardens.

Responding to this challenge

The alternative approach is to have shallow-plan dwellings with good square-shaped back gardens. They are placed back-to-back, in perimeter blocks, with secure private backs and frontage to the street. Road widths in front are the minimum consistent with the amount of traffic. In medium- to high-density areas, houses are terraced and, in low-density areas they are detached on spacious plots with space contained by trees. Ideally, buildings should be designed so that they can respond to the site. In other words, there should be real architecture. Failing this, dwelling types should, at least, be so designed that they can fit together easily to create satisfactory composition of urban form. Over a large area, such layouts can contain more dwellings and can, therefore, be more economic than the standard-volume house-builder product criticised earlier.

The first Essex design guide

Planning policies to implement this approach had their beginnings with the first *Essex design guide* (ECC, 1973) and in housing schemes that were built according to its principles on sites in many parts of that county. This document was not a brief policy statement but a book that tried to address broad issues of quality in residential design and to propose solutions. Its publication was a significant event. The guide made the point that, whatever the dreams of suburban living might be, the reality now fell well short of it. The analysis put forward by the guide focused in large part on townscape issues. Both the 'rural' situation, where space should be enclosed by trees, and the 'urban' situation, where space should be enclosed by buildings, could be visually satisfactory. The problem was that space was not being enclosed at all, and this was the principal reason why the suburban housing of the time was aesthetically unsatisfactory. It was unsatisfactory in many other ways as well, but this was the starting point of the analysis.

The real achievement of the design team within Essex County Council was that obtained in negotiation with the council's own engineers. As was common at the time, the highways standards required that roads should have standard widths and alignments, with footways on each side, in all circumstances. The design team succeeded in obtaining the engineers' agreement to significantly different designs where the amount of traffic was small. Why could not streets fronted by only a few houses have a shared surface? Why have a turning circle at the end of a cul-de-sac? There are very few houses there. Why not put it half way down, linked onwards by private drives? This would not only have aesthetic advantages but would also help developers by saving road costs. Unfortunately, the guide also recommended the use of layouts based on culs-de-sac. This was before traffic calming had been invented, and it appeared to be the only way of controlling traffic at the time. Aside from this issue, the scaling down of the width and alignment of access and feeder roads, together with the use of shared surfaces, where appropriate, remained one of the guide's most significant achievements.

What became a more controversial issue in some circles was the guide's advocacy of vernacular style and form. This was a principle that could trace its pedigree back to the beginnings of the Garden City Movement, notably the work of Parker and Unwin. The argument regarding style in the guide was that it should be specific to the locality. There should be a sense of place. Essex should look like Essex. The objective was to make urban areas look distinctive and the most straightforward way of achieving it was to start with themes based on vernacular architecture and local building materials. Vernacular architecture is something that changes over time, as buildings evolve to suit their location using local materials. Study of this process can therefore provide a lead into how to continue to make an area distinctive. It is, of course, both possible and desirable to interpret vernacular styles and materials in new and varied ways. Not only do people want modern conveniences to be incorporated, but reinvention and adaptation is part of the true essence of vernacular form.

This argument is, however, what made the guide controversial in some quarters. Whereas some architects saw it as an opportunity to be embraced, for others it touched a raw nerve and moved them to condemn the whole approach. There was both a belief that modernism represented the true spirit of the times and also that any guide would inhibit individuality and innovation. Against this, the point must be made that style is only one aspect of urban design. The greater part of the urban design process is not involved with style at all. When style is important, it is not a matter of personal taste. In the *Essex guide*, style was actively argued. It was rational argument. Moreover, the only realistic alternative choice available was the house builders' standard product. Speculative builders were not normally interested in new architectural ideas and did not construct modernist designs. Their product was a uniform one across the country and, aside from decorative fixtures, offered little scope for individual expression.

Some councils adopted the *Essex Guide* as policy, and others did not. What was interesting was that, even where the guide had not been adopted as policy, some architects and developers implemented it because they found it a more interesting approach. They could also get more houses in, and so it proved more, not less, profitable for them. Eventually the features of highway design that were to be found in the guide's approach became absorbed into national policy. Reductions in road widths and use of shared surfaces in residential design were endorsed by the government with the publication of *Design Bulletin 32* (DoE and DTp, 1977).

Towards the end of the 1970s, the design of schemes influenced by the guide was evolving. They were becoming a more urban expression of its principles. A notable example was the construction, in the late 1970s, of Noak Bridge, in Basildon, Essex, featured in the *Good Place Guide* (Billingham and Cole, 2002). Two architects working for the Basildon New Town Development Corporation, Maurice Naunton and George Garrard, who were designing New Town housing for rent, extended the interpretation of the guide. They designed a new pallet of house types, both houses and flats, that would facilitate continuous frontage. What resulted was a neovernacular urban form of considerable richness. The architects considered the result to be so successful that they left the service of the Development Corporation and pursued the project themselves with a local builder for sale to owner-occupiers. It is now difficult for visitors to see the difference between the rented housing and the housing built for sale. It showed where the *Essex design guide* could be taken and it anticipated the revision of the guide, and the more general design trends, of the 1990s.

West Dorset and Poundbury

What was, however, to become one of the most famous examples of the neovernacular approach did not occur in Essex but at Poundbury (Hardy, 2006), the urban extension to Dorchester in the County of Dorset. The scheme itself was promoted by the Prince of Wales through the Duchy of Cornwall, but the more general role of the local planning authority, West Dorset District Council, was also significant. Its own story paralleled that of Essex County Council and Chelmsford Borough Council in several ways including positive political leadership, co-operative working between stakeholders and innovative policies in design control.

In the 1980s, controversy had been caused in another part of the district by a housing development that local people had found incongruous. The chairman of the planning committee took this matter up as a general issue with the council's officers and received support from David Oliver, the council's chief architect. Support was also obtained from the Dorset County Council for more sympathetic and flexible highway standards. The result was a policy line that promoted a more traditional design philosophy, drawing upon the Dorset vernacular, for infill in towns and villages (Hardy, 2006).

The District Council also needed to provide for significantly more housing and proposed an extension to Dorchester to accommodate it. What would normally have happened in such circumstances is that, after the District Council had allocated this land for housing, it would have been sold by its owners to house builders. The council would then attempt to control the design of these houses through the planning process. In this case, however, all the land was owned by the Duchy of Cornwall, who decided to use their ownership to control the development and thereby obtain high standards of design even though the properties would eventually be sold off to residents.

Prince Charles turned for advice to the urbanist and architect Leon Krier and the urban designer and civil engineer Alan Baxter, who were commissioned to prepare a master plan setting out the blocks and urban spaces. Their layout embodied a mix of uses with shops, offices and small workshops closely integrated with the housing. Continuous active frontage, with buildings close to the street and with small gardens behind, was the norm. Streets allowed access by car but were not designed around the car. The original ideas for style had a strong classical flavour. However, as a result of planning consultations, especially those with the public, this was replaced by an approach based more on the Dorset vernacular. The three-dimensional architectural style was overseen by David Oliver. Although he later left the service of the council and became a consultant to the Duchy, the Duchy and District Council policies remained in harmony.

What was significant was the way in which a number of parties, landowners, local councils, local politicians and professionals came together. This was not limited to Poundbury but became characteristic of the council's general approach to design control. Although Poundbury was the most sizeable and famous example, it was not alone amongst the interesting new housing schemes in West Dorset. In 2003, the District Council, in addition to Chelmsford and Cambridge, was awarded Beacon Status for the Quality of the Built Environment by the central government.

The revision of the Essex design guide

Poundbury had been conceived in the late 1980s, and building had started in the early 1990s. During this period, thinking on urban design had continued to advance. The publication in 1985 of *Responsive Environments* (Bentley et al., 1985) had provided both a coherent argument for, and practical guide to, this growing trend. Its impact as a textbook for numerous urban designers in the years that followed (including the author) should not be underestimated.

In Essex, during this period, innovative housing schemes, reflecting the trends in design thinking, continued to be built although they were more isolated examples than a general trend. Notable amongst them was the strong urban scheme at Gate Street, Maldon, by Mel Dunbar, constructed in 1994–1995.

The pressing need to revise the *Essex design guide* had been clear for some time. This lengthy, and much delayed, process eventually took place during the early 1990s. The new guide (EPOA, 1997) was finally approved and published in 1997. The most important change was the replacement of cul-de-sacs by grid-type road layouts. The other significant improvement was to tighten up on the criteria for 'urban' form, drawing, as one example, upon the housing at Gate Street, Maldon. Continuous frontages were required at densities above 20 dph. As most standard house buildings at that time were at 20–25 dph, the guide required, in practice, that nearly all the volume house-builder dwellings exhibit continuous frontage. Shallow-plan houses, easy to light and ventilate naturally and with good-sized rear gardens, were required. By placing the garage in the back garden, accessed though an archway from the front, two cars could easily be accommodated without putting them on the street. The result was a strong urban form. As the houses were closer to the street, higher overall density could also be obtained.

A national policy

As the 1990s progressed, the pressure for higher quality in design merged with thinking on the desirability of more sustainable development. Both trends began to be incorporated into statements of policy by the British government (DETR, 1998a). Much of this was motivated by the need to accommodate increasing numbers of dwellings with minimum public opposition. This was seen as requiring higher densities and greater use of previously developed land. Government policy eventually sought the raising of residential densities to at least 30 dph. To be successful, this required both an 'urban' character and uniformly higher design standards.

Whatever the actual motivation, the support for planning intervention in pursuit of design quality increased dramatically. Back in 1992, the British government had published the second edition of *Design Bulletin 32* (DoE and DTp, 1992) updating and reinforcing the original argument. In 1998, this document's urban design implications were expanded upon by *Places, Streets and Movement* (DETR, 1998b). From 2000 onwards, the approach to residential design described here was to be reflected by nearly all the guides sponsored by the British government and advice by the Commission for Architecture and the Built Environment. In 2000, the urban design message was stated in a concise, but coherent, form in *By Design* (DETR and CABE, 2000). In the same year, English Partnerships published their *Urban Design Compendium* (Davies and English Partnerships & the Housing Corporation, 2000), that remains one of the most useful and practical of guides. These guides were followed in 2001 by *Better Places to Live* (DTLR and CABE, 2001) and the many subsequent documents that reinforced the same theme.

An urban renaissance?

The beginning of the 1990s saw increasingly frequent debates in planning and architectural circles about the desirability of getting people to live once more at higher densities in the centres of cities. This controversy had, of course, been of very long standing, arising originally from reaction to suburbanisation and counter-urbanisation in North America epitomised by the writings in the 1960s of Lewis Mumford and Jane Jacobs, on one side, and Herbert Gans and Melvin Webber, on the other. However, in 1990s Britain, the increasing demand for housing, and opposition to the building of it by the public, had been an ever-growing problem. Opposition to house building had been perceived as arising from building on greenfield sites, and building in towns, so it was believed, might be easier to achieve politically. Also, less infrastructure might need to be provided, reducing overall costs. It had been noted that people did live in city centres in many other European countries. Could the English be persuaded to accept this, in spite of their clear preference to living in the countryside? This was to lead to the Labour Government, from 1997 onwards, pursuing the question actively and setting up the Urban Task Force to advance its aims, resulting in the publication of *Towards an Urban Renaissance* (UTF, 1999) and *Our Towns and Cities: The Future – Delivering an Urban Renaissance* (DETR, 2000).

It remains entirely likely that the great majority of the British population would prefer to live in the countryside if it were feasible, which, unfortunately, it can never be for all of them. The same would apply, no doubt, in many other countries. On the other hand, there has always been a significant minority who wish to live in, or near, city centres. Here they can enjoy a wide range of amenities, especially those catering to minority cultural tastes, within a very short distance. Not only this, but, demographically, the proportion of the population for whom such a lifestyle is desirable, small households with high incomes (both young people and active 'empty-nesters'), has been increasing. Town-centre living is also appropriate for those with special needs, notably older people, who also form an increasing proportion of the total population.

The issue was, in reality, not so much a matter of preferences as one of land values. From the mid-1960s onwards, people had not been able to obtain dwellings in city centres (other than parts of central London) even if they had wanted to. This was because office uses possessed the highest land values and were driving residential uses out. However, after the end of the office boom in the late 1980s, the demand started to fall, especially for large single-user facilities. By the 1990s, residential uses possessed the highest values. It took developers some years to realise that changes were taking place. However, once they had understood it, they wanted to build only high-density housing in town centres. In many cases, redundant office blocks were converted into flats. The demand for city-centre living from people who were able to pay for it was, in reality, very high.

An urban renaissance was not something, therefore, to be imposed upon a reluctant populace but something for developers and planning authorities to facilitate. It could, though, easily be obstructed. With lack of vision, low-intensity uses could be allowed on vacant brownfield land so that, by the time the potential for high-density high-value development was perceived, the land was no longer available. Another obstacle was that planning policies requiring the retention of 'employment land' did not permit the release of redundant industrial land in, and around, town centres. The post-industrial economy did not require the same amount of floor space as the original manufacturing activities, creating a potential supply of 'brownfield land'. During the 1980s, low-intensity retail and leisure uses were permitted on such land by the government of the day. In the 1990s, government policy changed and these uses were discouraged. Nevertheless, development plan requirements frequently required that existing 'employment land' be retained and more provided. In this context, the term 'employment land' included manufacturing and warehousing but excluded shopping centres, universities, hospitals and such like, even though these uses were often the principal sources of employment. In parts of southeast England, at least, this had the ironic effect of creating a regeneration problem where none should have existed. The economy at large did not need regenerating, but there were large areas of land in the central locations that were now standing derelict awaiting 'employment' uses that were not going to return. They either accommodated new distribution facilities or the land lay unused. They were, however, being preserved from low-intensity retail uses while being kept available for an 'urban renaissance' once such policies became a reality.

In reality, the influx of people into a town provided the motor that reinvigorated the local economy by providing new sources of employment. The new residents bought with them a demand for quality shops and other services. Changing technology meant that it could be economical to have city-centre shops selling high-quality durable goods that could be delivered to customers' homes. This was also being extended to groceries. There was also a demand and readiness to pay for restaurants and entertainment, which became an ever-growing source of both services and employment.

An unlikely high achiever?

The recommendations in this book arise from responses to these challenges. They were developed through practical experience in a typical large English town, Chelmsford, Essex. For anyone interested in how significant long-term improvements in urban design can be achieved, the Chelmsford story can be an interesting one. This interest stems from a dramatic turnaround that took place in the late 1990s. What had been an average and unprepossessing town had become one that was liveable and sophisticated. A substantive and continuing urban renaissance had begun. Whereas, for many, the town may not have been seen as in any way remarkable in terms of professional practice, by 2003 it was clearly in the forefront. High standards of design had become the norm across the Borough, a position recognised by the award of Beacon Status for the Quality of the Built Environment by the government in 2003. This good practice was also attested to studies by the Commission for Architecture and the Built Environment, including their *Housing Audit* (CABE, 2004). The town even achieved an entry in the *Good Place Guide* (Billingham and Cole, 2002).

The experience in Chelmsford showed how the gradual increase over time of both the quantity of published policy, and its degree of prescription, resulted in better quality of architecture and a more vibrant public realm. It is not something that should be seen as peculiar to Chelmsford or to the period in question. It has wide applicability. Chelmsford was very typical of many towns within the more prosperous parts of northwest Europe and other parts of the developed world. Because it had not been particularly well endowed, by British standards, with architectural heritage, its experiences could be seen as all the more relevant to other planning authorities. If this town could do it, then why not others?

Chelmsford town has a population of approximately 100 000 and is situated 50 km northeast of London in the centre of the County of Essex. Much of the 20th century urban development of south and central Essex is rather uninspiring, usually seen as the butt of jokes rather than as a beacon of achievement. In Chelmsford during the 1960s and 1970s, redevelopment was far from satisfactory. Although then a comparatively modest market town, it experienced substantial reconstruction of its town centre and continual suburban expansion. Developments of very poor design and the loss of historic buildings and townscape caused resentment amongst local people. Industrial restructuring was leading to abandoned manufacturing sites in and near the town centre that were in need of regeneration. There was concern about the growing competition from out-of-town and edge-of-town shopping centres. In the eyes of many, Chelmsford would have been an unlikely candidate for eventual Beacon Status.

Nevertheless, it had continued to grow and prosper and urban development was still proceeding at a significant rate. As a result of both government and county council policies, Chelmsford was subject to a substantial and ongoing house-building programme and increases in population. Decline in manufacturing industry had been more than compensated for by the expansion of service employment. The town had been especially fortunate in the location of most of its jobs, and its bus and railway stations, in the town centre. The expansion of shopping in the town centre, which had appeared resilient to out-of-town competition, gave further impetus to the positive direction of growth. The fact that the cycle of development was ongoing and proceeding at a substantial pace had always offered the prospect of a better future, if only the development process could be properly steered.

In 1996, a new political administration started the process of achieving higher standards of design and sustainability in the built environment. The first significant changes to planning policies came in 1997. Not only was a Borough-wide Local Plan (CBC, 1997a) finally adopted but the council also adopted the revised *Essex design guide* (EPOA, 1997) as supplementary planning guidance. These two events provided a foundation from which further progress in design control in the Borough could be made. The guide, in particular, was part of the process of providing clear and positive guidance to developers. The process of creating a more effective structure for the council's operations was also begun, at both officer and political levels, including the creation of team of professional urban designers.

As Chelmsford entered the new millennium, the position was reached where every development was expected to achieve the required standards. New spatial policy that made its physical implications explicit was published (CBC, 2001a). The council's urban design team was approaching its full strength of five professionals and was applying its accumulated experience in negotiation to each proposal that came forward. As the staffing position on urban design gradually improved, so the rate of production of detailed site-specific briefs increased. The degree of prescription and delineation of desired physical structure also increased. Each site where major development was expected now had a design brief well in advance, which outlined the location of blocks, identifying the perimeter block form and the location and character of urban spaces.

There was also a change to the corporate culture, with greater inter-professional working. By 2002, all major development proposals were handled by a team of an urban designer, development control case officer, traffic engineer and such other professional from arboriculture, law, housing, parks and leisure as might have been relevant. Overall, this turnaround took 6 years to achieve. This was a considerable task that was not just a matter of policy content but also of resources and process.

A proactive approach

This book sets out a way of building urban design into the local planning process, based on actual experiences of turning around the built form and urban life of a town by both political and professional means. It relates how design ideas can be translated into day-to-day practice. This is a significant challenge for any town or city. It requires looking at different ways of expressing what planners do and getting away from the usual job descriptions in their bureaucratic context.

Urban design is not normally a statutorily required function of a planning authority. However, embracing it as a planning activity radically changes the way a local authority approaches the statutory processes of plan making and controlling development. It creates the potential for improving spatial policy. Place making can become a basis for requiring quality through planning approvals. All the planning tools at a local council's disposal have potentially huge scope for positive, creative influence, through briefing, policy statements and agreements.

In human terms, all this is not necessarily easy. It often means overcoming resistance from the development industry, professional cynicism and a tendency to neglect the details of design. There are a number of potential obstacles in the way of design-led planning. First, the development industry can operate on the basis of standard product, the rule of the sales department and a constant review of build costs. Second, planning can collide with other processes. Affordable housing design may have to be negotiated before a housing provider is on board. The specification and adoption of highways can unpick design quality. Professional cynicism can threaten positive values. After permission had been granted, amendments can be made, quality watered down, architects changed and ransom strips retained. There can be neglect of approval of details. It is very easy for a planning authority to pay insufficient attention to details. Finally, it can be threatened by a performance culture where speed of decision could easily dominate the attainment of quality outcomes.

In practical terms, a local planning authority's urban design role is promotional. It does not design the built environment as such, but anticipates and encourages development, influencing and guiding those who make the investment. A local council's role is to set the place-making objectives based on an understanding of the strategic picture and of site opportunities. This means it is sometimes leading, sometimes partnering and at other times scrutinising.

Ultimately, achieving well-located, well-designed places depends on how the local planning authority works with developers for particular sites. For major developments, planning authorities and developers are simultaneously both partners and opponents. Local councils are promoting and enabling development while, at the same time, challenging and negotiating its form and content. This tension is an essential part of achieving better quality and the aim should be to make the most of this relationship.

This requires an approach that it is *proactive*, in contrast to the *reactive* stance often associated with control of development. Being proactive requires

- belief – being evangelical about good places;
- vision – anticipating and analysing;
- being positive about development – promoting opportunities and creative ideas;
- being active – influencing, demonstrating and facilitating;
- taking risks – innovating and pushing the scope of policy and control;
- understanding site and context;
- choosing the right means of influence;
- fighting the clock.

It is an activity that is design-led, opportunity-led, objective-focused and outcome-oriented. The key elements necessary for achieving a proactive approach are

- sound design principles;
- published policy and briefs;
- investment in staff and co-operative working.

Design principles

Design principles should ensure that new development creates a sense of place, respects its context and meets functional needs. The overall aim should be to make places by envisaging, shaping and managing change. It means thinking of places and communities at different spatial levels – the town, the neighbourhood, and the street – taking account of the physical and intangible qualities that go to make a place. Making places involves specifying location and linkages, uses and density and the context for the design of buildings. Routes, spaces and perimeter blocks lie at the heart of successful design. Buildings should face outwards and contain space. The quality of the public realm should be used to glue a whole place together. Making places seeks to integrate usable green spaces into new places. It aims to 'lose the road' in good shared surfaces, treating highway design as part of the landscape architecture.

Published policy

Published policy enables all parties in the development process to know the position of the planning authority at an early stage and to know it clearly. It has two components:

- a clear physically based spatial strategy;
- briefs for all significant sites.

A physically based spatial strategy

A physically based spatial strategy for a town is needed to relate the intensity of development to accessibility, in pursuit of the reduction of the need to travel, and travel by sustainable modes. These accessibility principles lead logically to the promotion of an urban renaissance involving the intensive use of town-centre brownfield land. They also lead to the need for access to open green areas, both within the redeveloped areas and through 'green corridors' linking them to the suburbs and countryside. They need to embody a long-term vision, especially in the town centre. Achievement of more intensive development and an urban renaissance requires not just a vision of new physical form but also an understanding of how this will be facilitated by the increase of land values over time.

The planning brief

The planning brief is the foundation of the proactive approach and the principal vehicle for setting out design expectations for a site. Where development is anticipated, or is being promoted by a planning authority, planning briefs set out principles and guide design. They often help to unlock complex urban sites. If done quickly, they influence value, increase certainty and establish a design approach before negotiation takes place. Different types of brief can be devised to suit different circumstances: area-wide strategies for regeneration areas, frameworks for groups of sites, planning briefs for sites, master plans for large development areas and concept statements to lead site layout. In each case, the aim should be to put design at the heart of the process and to convey clearly the urban design objectives. Briefs should be short with clear graphic presentation. Although they can cover a variety of formats, all should provide unambiguous guidance on physical form, including specification of blocks and frontages.

Investment in staff

All this cannot be achieved without investment in sufficient staff with the required expertise. Not only is an urban design team of professionals needed but a proactive process requires co-operative working, as opposed to merely consulting, both between the different professions within a planning authority and with the agencies involved in the development process.

The structure of the book

The book is set out in two parts. The first part deals with the nature of the recommended proactive approach. The first chapter sets out the changes to organisational structure and culture that are needed. The second chapter describes how urban design can, and should, be integrated with broader spatial policy. The preparation of physically prescriptive guides, briefs and master plans is dealt with in the third chapter. The fourth chapter describes, with examples, how higher standards of design can be achieved through proactive negotiation. The second part of the book describes how the proactive approach evolved at Chelmsford and gives examples of what was achieved on the ground.

The story of how higher standards of residential design were achieved is related in the fifth chapter. The sixth and seventh chapters describe the achievement of an urban renaissance in the town centre, the former dealing with improvements to the commercial life and the public realm in the town centre and the later, with the return of people to live there.

Part One

A Proactive Approach

Chapter 1

Getting organised

Urban design is not an activity that can be pursued in isolation from other aspects of the planning process or from the functioning of the development industry. Achieving urban design outcomes is a pluralist activity. Although there is a place for the preparation of detailed designs for large areas by individuals or small groups, this is, in reality, a rare event. Within planning authorities, urban design is part of a wider planning function comprising many different activities and skills. The planning activity is, in turn, one of a number of local government services that influence physical form and structure. All these are regulated, ideally led, by a political process. For their part, developers engage in a range of activities and skills within their organisations and engage the services of a range of professional consultants. The quality of the final outcome stems from the nature of the interaction of these groups over a period of time. To be effective, any urban design process must recognise and embrace this complexity.

The process is not just pluralistic but also incremental. The acquisition of land, and the acquiring of permission to develop, is a step-by-step process. For urban design to be successful, it must embrace this fact also and recognise that design is situated within an ongoing process of control. For its part, planning control must recognise that it must embrace the creative nature of the urban design process.

The role of vision

A sense of vision is essential to a proactive approach. In this context, it is not something vague or abstract but practical, a manifestation of conviction. The purpose of planning is to deal with uncertainty. It does this by setting out policies that will endure over a given period of time and thus provide the means of coping with unexpected circumstances. The actual proposals should stem from these policies. The difficulty in planning (as with all other aspects of government) is to implement them. This results, unfortunately but unavoidably, in a long, drawn-out process.

Analysis of past experience is essential in order to learn from mistakes and understand the processes at work. Where vision takes over is in providing the basis for the proper articulation of goals and policies in such a way that a picture of what is desired emerges. Attention can then be focused on understanding the path to achieving it. In other words, vision applies not only to future end states but also to process and, moreover, to a conviction that the end can eventually be achieved. In the context of proactive urban design, this means that not only must there be a clear view of what good design would mean in physical terms, but also a strong conviction that, over time, it is realisable.

This is illustrated by the pursuit of an urban renaissance in Chelmsford described in Chapter 6. In 1995, this goal did not appear amongst the council's policies, and movement towards it was not discernible on the ground. Some developers were proposing low-intensity shopping and commercial schemes. None was promoting housing in the town centre. Vision was needed not only to see what the town centre could be like, and the advantages it would bring socially and economically, but also to realise that economic and demographic processes were working in this direction. If higher-intensity uses were to be encouraged, then this would bring about a rise in land values that would make further development of this type more and more profitable and attractive. A virtuous circle would be created. On the other hand, permitting low-intensity uses would block the achievement of an urban renaissance for many decades to come by using up the available brownfield sites. The vision was also important in perceiving changes in central government policy and predicting how they would develop. Merely looking at past policy and doing what was done before would not have delivered the goods. It is worth noting that Chelmsford's change of direction began before the promotion by the central government of an urban renaissance. *Towards an Urban Renaissance* (UTF, 1999), for example, was not published until 1999.

Building a design team

A central tenet of the proactive approach is that there is no substitute for the possession of in-house expertise. However, what is important is both the number of professional urban designers and also the way they are used. Although a team may work on its own initiative on some projects, it should not be conceived of as a separate 'design section' that works separately from the other planning operations and is only involved with them when consulted. It must work together with all other planning operations and to take the lead for major developments. It must also work closely with other council services, especially housing, parks, leisure and engineering. The activities of a design team would include

- negotiations on major developments, with both internal and external parties, before, during and after consideration of planning applications;

and the writing of

- briefs, an ongoing task that takes up most of the officer's time;
- character appraisals for conservation areas and other sites;
- policy for development plans.

This list cannot, however, convey the complexity of the actual day-to-day operations as the aforementioned items tend to interact with each other and the work on them tends to blend together.

The Chelmsford team

At its full strength, the Chelmsford design team consisted of five professional urban designers: one team manager, one principal officer, one senior officer and two junior officers. Within the hierarchy, the manager reported to the head of planning services, although this statement does not convey the complexity of interaction that characterised the actual operation of the team and its interactions within the corporate structure.

The setting up of the design team, as part of the creation of new patterns of expertise within the wider officer corps, was a rather prosaic example of the application of vision. Making personnel changes is notoriously difficult. However, if there is a clear idea of what is to be achieved, then the vision can guide appointments as vacancies arise. At Chelmsford, once a clear view of the need for the number of urban designers had been established, building up the design team could be achieved over time. If there had been no clear view of the expertise profile required, or if it had been re-debated and amended every time there was a vacancy to be filled, then the emergence of the team would have been unlikely, to say the least.

Co-operative working

Chelmsford had a development control section under a manager who reported to the head of planning services. There were specialist officers for listed buildings, landscape and arboriculture. There was a development plan section also under a manager. During the time period covered by this book, the Borough Council had separate services for engineering, economic development, strategic housing, parks, leisure and law, all of which interacted to varying degrees with the planning function.

For small-sized, and some medium-sized, developments, the initiative would lie with the development control case officer, who would bring in the design team as appropriate. However, for all large-scale, and some medium-scale, developments, the initiative was with the design team. The development control case officer was then an essential and important member the team. However, the urban design officer would have written a brief, in anticipation of any proposal arising, and would have started discussions with other services as part of the process. When an application for planning permission was imminent, the development control case officer and other appropriate planning officers would start to make their contributions to the corporate process. Very significant developments would be discussed with the head of planning services, deputy chief executive and executive (cabinet) member responsible for planning. Such liaison would continue throughout until the building had been constructed. A particular characteristic of Chelmsford's approach, during the period covered by this book, was that an engineer officer would work closely with the urban design and development control officers on the detailed design. These three would form the core of the team that would reach out to other specialist planning staff, other services, chief officers and councillors as appropriate. The interest of the design team would not cease once the buildings had been constructed; it would continue to have an interest in how development proceeded and was monitored afterwards. Matters of enforcement, though, would be a matter for the seperat enforcement section.

Political leadership

Whether or not political support is forthcoming for design control can depend on how public opinion bears upon local councillors. The public's attitude can be changed by its experience of planning outcomes. If people can see good results on the ground, this will work into the political process. This is something that can be very important, in the long term, for support for particular design policies.

A rather uncommon characteristic of the Chelmsford story was that it was initiated at elected member level, and by a councillor who was also a professional planner. People have often asked if this had been problematic for the professional planning officers. Whatever may or may not have been the case in the 1996–1997 period, by 2002 it was clear that the changes that occurred had brought the professional reputation of the planning authority from being rather unremarkable to greater prominence, arguably to the leading edge of planning practice. Would this leadership from councillors be a necessary part of any improvement elsewhere? Certainly, support by councillors is essential and leadership at this level is extremely valuable. Chelmsford appointed a 'design champion' at council member level as well as one at officer level. All the local planning authorities short-listed for Beacon Status for the Quality of the Built Environment demonstrated it. Their presentation teams all included at least one leading council member, and it is difficult to believe that any local planning authority could have achieved the Beacon Status without it. On the other hand, it would clearly be undesirable if it were a necessary condition, as then progress might occur only rarely. The ideal situation would be one in which councillors are committed to achieving a quality environment, fund the appointment of staff with the requisite skills and then give these officers their full support.

The arrangements at Chelmsford

Political leadership is not just a strategic issue but something that is experienced in more routine arrangements. At Chelmsford, all planning guidance, in particular the site-specific briefs, were approved by the Borough Council executive (later cabinet) on behalf of the council. The guidance was presented to the executive by the executive member responsible for planning. In effect, this gave the executive member considerable control over the content of the guidance, for if he did not approve it personally, it would not be presented to the executive. If a site became available for development unexpectedly, or at short notice, then officers would prepare a concept statement that would be issued to the prospective developers without political approval. The text of the document would make it clear that it did not legally commit the council. If the decision-making process subsequently dragged on for some time, then the document would be taken through the political process so as to give it the official status of supplementary planning guidance. In the event of an appeal, it would then carry greater weight.

Political involvement in the process for determining applications for planning permission was quite different. Although decisions on 90% of planning applications were delegated to officers, the volume of major applications was such that this left a considerable number to be determined by members of the council. This was handled by a monthly planning committee under its own chairman.

Whereas the process for handling planning applications was fairly standard, the process for deciding more strategic spatial policy, especially statutory development plans, was more distinctive. A great deal of work was done by a small panel of members of the council drawn from all political parties. This panel met with chief officers, and other officers doing the detailed work, to discuss the content of the policy as it was drawn up. This proved invaluable for a number of reasons. One was that the issues were highly complex and poring over them in small groups meant that not only would time be saved in public debate but that better decisions were made in the long run. Both officers and members could express themselves more frankly and objectively in private and informal setting. Many of the issues were highly contentious and private discussion not only meant that they could be handled more objectively, but also that potentially divisive topics could be identified at an early stage.

Once the panel had done all it could, the draft policy would be presented by officers to the Development Policy Board. This was a fairly large committee of councillors that included the executive member for planning and, normally, the chairman of the planning committee, but which also had its own separate chairman. The chairman of the Development Policy Board was also one of the leading members of the council in regard to planning issues and would join with the executive member for planning in discussions with chief officers as appropriate. The Development Policy Board discussed the draft policy publicly, but separately, from the deliberations of both the executive and the planning committee. It had, however, no delegated decision-making powers and its conclusions were presented to the full council for final debate and decision. Matters relating to statutory development plans were always reserved for the decision of the full council.

A change of attitude

Consider the difference between the following two modes of thinking and what it means for planning authorities dealing with major complex proposals.

First, that connected with urban design could be categorised as conceptual, holistic and instinctive. It seeks distinctive solutions and to master the whole picture before attending to detail. On the other hand, development control thinking could be categorised as practical, categorising and rational. It seeks tried-and-tested solutions and to master the detail of each topic prior to assembling the whole. For urban design to be effective, the latter must embrace the former. To quote from *Towards an Urban Renaissance*,

> A strategic planning system regards land use planning as a positive mechanism for achieving change, particularly urban regeneration objectives, rather than, primarily, a reactive means of controlling development.
>
> A flexible planning system responds to the needs of different places in different ways, and rewards higher quality development with faster and less conditional permissions. (UTF, 1999)

The experience at Chelmsford was that there were development control practitioners who were keen to work in a positive manner, once the institutional environment encouraged and supported it. It was essential to appoint professional staff with the correct expertise and to facilitate cooperative working, not merely mutual consultation, between them and planning colleagues. All this required support at the political level. Indeed, at Chelmsford, it stemmed from the political leadership. Once this had been achieved, it was possible to establish a more creative development control ethos that aspired to the following ways of thinking:

- an attitude of mind that opens possibilities;
- problem solving based on open-minded thinking;
- taking of intellectual risks;
- approaching problems afresh;
- questioning rather than criticising;
- rewriting procedures;
- an integrated, holistic view.

The result was a *proactive approach* that exhibited:

- *belief* – being evangelical about good places;
- *vision* – anticipating trends;
- *positive* – thinking about development;

and was

- *opportunity led* – objective focused and outcome oriented;
- *active* – influencing, demonstrating and facilitating;
- *taking risks* – innovating, widening the scope of policy and control.

Chapter 2

Urban design as spatial policy

A vision of a well-designed town or city has to be delivered, in part, through the spatial policies within development plans at the town and city level. It is fallacious to imagine that the strategic and the more detailed treatments of the physical form of an urban area can be handled as though they were completely separate operations, or to believe that one would determine the other as a simple consequence. The same applies to the separation of physical form and land-use, at least in the short term. Not only do the physical consequence of the pursuit of more strategic spatial objectives need to be spelt out, but an understanding of urban design principles needs to be fed into the preparation of these spatial policies. In other words, although the final presentation of a development plan may proceed from the general to the particular, and from the strategic to the detailed, an understanding of what is desired in physical form is necessary for the formulation of the goals, objectives and locational principles in the plan. Both general design principles and place-specific policies are situated within wider spatial policy.

In other words, planning activities at different spatial scales cannot operate independently of each other. The aspect of policy where this is particularly noticeable is the pursuit of sustainability. Local actions by individuals connect through to phenomena at a global scale, such as climate change, with implications at all the scales in between. Likewise, physical planning cannot be divorced from the pursuit of sustainability and cannot be pursued at a local level in isolation from more strategic spatial policy. It is, for example, connected directly to the provision of transport infrastructure, something that has implications at a regional scale.

This is not just a matter of scale but of time horizon. Urban design is concerned with the physical form and structure of urban areas. This form and structure can persist over very long periods of time, far longer than the uses of land that may, in comparison, seem ephemeral. Urban design initiatives have significance way beyond the informing of short-term negotiations. Physical planning is, therefore, at the heart of spatial planning and so, in consequence, is urban design.

An understanding of design

Establishing a clear and common understanding of what is meant by 'urban design' is needed at the outset. It is a core problem-solving activity that determines the quality of the built environment. Its goal is the meeting of basic human needs for security and sociability. As a process, urban design is a means of organising space. This involves making connections, organising activity, relating to surroundings, integrating with the existing urban pattern and creating visual order. Ultimately, it requires getting development to work.

The overall goal should be making places. A planning authority should envisage, shape and manage change to this end. It should think of places and communities at different spatial levels: the town, the neighbourhood and the street, taking account of the physical and intangible qualities that make a place. The role of urban design in making sense of these qualities is expressed in plans and development decisions. It involves specifying location, linkages, uses, densities and the context for the design of buildings.

In essence, it is important to

- ensure that new development has its own identity – make it *this* place not that place;
- make this character derive from the local landscape and local culture;
- connect one place to another place directly, to make it easy to walk from here to there;
- ensure the placing of buildings helps people to find their way;
- make sure that what is built is fit for the future and can adapt to household, community and lifestyle changes over the years;
- make sure places have diverse uses, diverse people and are active through the day.

In the case of Britain, these qualities are now, fortunately, to be found within the government guidance for practitioners. The publication *By Design* (DETR and CABE, 2000) translated them into a convenient summary of urban design objectives that can inform planning policy of any local planning authority, as set out in Table 2.1. Significantly, *By Design* adds two more objectives to this list. One is about using buildings to enclose space, making buildings lines flow continuously to make streets, containing public space and secluding private areas. The other is about good space, making sure that the spaces between buildings through which people move are useful, safe, visible and pleasant to be in.

Goals, objectives and locational principles

A development plan should be firmly based in the goals of sustainability and quality of life. Principles of spatial organisation can be deduced from these goals and thence more detailed physical planning criteria. Examples of

Table 2.1 Urban design objectives from By Design (DETR and CABE, 2000).

Objectives of urban design

Character
A place with its own identity | To promote character in townscape and landscape by responding to and reinforcing locally distinctive patterns of development, landscape and culture

Continuity and enclosure
A place where public and private spaces are clearly distinguished | To promote the continuity of street frontages and the enclosure of space by development that clearly defines private and public areas

Quality of the public realm
A place with attractive and successful outdoor areas | To promote public spaces and routes that are attractive, safe, uncluttered and work effectively for all in society, including disabled and elderly people

Ease of movement
A place that is easy to get to and move through | To promote accessibility and local permeability by making places that connect with each other and are easy to move through, putting people before traffic and integrating land uses and transport

Legibility
A place that has a clear image and is easy to understand | To promote legibility through development that provides recognisable routes, intersections and landmarks to help people find their way around

Adaptability
A place that can change easily | To promote adaptability through development that can respond to changing social, technological and economic conditions

Diversity
A place with variety and choice | To promote diversity and choice through a mix of compatible developments and uses that work together to create viable places that respond to local needs

Source: Reproduced under HMSO PSI licence C2006011221.

goals and objectives developed at Chelmsford* are shown in Table 2.2. The general locational principles to follow from this statement were those shown in Box 2.1. They not only promoted biodiversity, mixed uses and preference for brownfield sites, but, most importantly, also required a sustainable pattern of development based on access to transport nodes and local facilities.

*At Chelmsford, during the period covered by this book, the principal vehicle for spatial policy was the Borough Plan 2001–2011 (CBC, 2001a). It went on deposit in 2001 and thus became, legally, a material consideration for the determination of applications for planning provision. Although it was, unfortunately, withdrawn in 2003 for political reasons, its policies were used in the determination of planning applications for a 2-year period and applied to many of the developments discussed in this book.

Table 2.2 Example of plan goals and objectives.

Goals	Objectives
Social progress that recognises the needs of everyone.	To ensure the provision of types and tenures of dwelling that meet the needs of the whole community, including affordable and special needs housing. To help alleviate poverty and social exclusion in areas of particular need. To ensure increased accessibility of services to all sectors of the community, particularly for people who are disabled or older and those in receipt of benefits. To encourage a healthy lifestyle. To enhance leisure opportunities. To reduce crime and the fear of crime.
Facilitating the restructuring and enhancement of the local economy.	To ensure the provision of land, buildings and transport systems to respond to the changing character of the local economy.
Prudent use of natural resources and protection of the environment.	To protect and encourage biodiversity. To be economical with the consumption of land and efficient in the use of land. To reduce fossil-fuel-based energy consumption. To reduce pollution and waste. To conserve and make accessible open green space. To enhance the built and landscape heritage.
Encourage the provision, co-ordination and integration of all modes of transport in the interests of sustainability, accessibility and safety.	To pursue a co-ordinated transport system to meet the economic and social needs of the town. To improve accessibility for all, particularly to jobs, shopping, leisure facilities and services by public transport, walking and cycling. To improve safety on the transport network and personal security of users. To integrate the transport strategy with the development plan. To reduce the adverse environmental impact of transport. To reduce the need to travel, especially by car.
A high quality of built development for the people of the town.	To ensure urban areas are integrated, accessible, attractive, secure and functional.

Source: Chelmsford Borough Council.

They were given detailed substance by the locational principles shown in Box 2.2. Effectively, all major new development was to be contained within 800 m walking-distance of the town centre, or other centres around new, or existing, public transport interchanges, creating what are known as *pedestrian-sheds* (*ped-shed* for short). The transport nodes had to be on an established public transport corridor. There is a high degree of correspondence here to *transit-oriented developments,* to use a term familiar in New Urbanist circles.

Box 2.1   Examples of general locational principles.

Sustainable Locations for New Development

The Council will promote and secure sustainable development throughout the Borough. In allocating land for development, account will be taken of the following sustainability criteria:

1. Making the best use of previously developed land within the urban areas, particularly close to their centres, and using a design-led approach to optimise the potential of individual sites.
2. Creating sustainable patterns of development by relating new development to public transport nodes and local facilities, and encouraging integrated transport initiatives.
3. Encouraging mixed-use development, incorporating housing, retail and business uses and new leisure and recreation opportunities.
4. Protecting and promoting biodiversity in all development proposals.
5. Phasing the release of development sites in order that previously used sites within the urban areas and rural settlements are released ahead of any 'greenfield' sites.

Source: Chelmsford Borough Council.

Box 2.2   Examples of detailed locational principles.

Locating Development to Reduce the Need to Travel

In meeting the requirements for new development allocations in the plan period, and thereafter, the council will require all proposals for major new development to have regard to the need to reduce travel. With that aim, the council will apply the following priority to proposed locations:

Priority-One Locations: Development within the central area of a major urban centre.

Priority-Two Locations: Development within 800 m walking-distance of a major urban centre.

Priority-Three Locations: Development within 800 m of a neighbourhood centre that contains centrally located key facilities, including a public transport interchange with frequent public transport services to a major urban centre along an established public transport corridor.

Planning permission will be refused for development proposals that do not fall within these categories.

Limits on the Size of Major New Mixed-Use 'Greenfield' Developments

The physical extent of major new mixed-use 'greenfield' development will be limited by a comfortable walking-distance of 800 m from the major public transport interchanges and the centrally located key local facilities serving that development.

Source: Chelmsford Borough Council.

Intensity of development

For a wide range of reasons, especially those connected with the pursuit of sustainability, planning policies and arguments in many parts of the world call for higher residential densities. However, high density should not seen as an end in itself. Although fulfilling some important policies, it has its own disadvantages. The higher the density, the costlier is the construction. It is not advantageous, in itself, to have apartments instead of houses. It works against the pursuit of sustainability. In addition, in any urban context there will be limits to the density that can be achieved. It is constrained by housing mix, external space needs and local scale and form.

The term 'high density' can possess a wide range of meanings. There is the 'more than 30 dph' of British government policy since at least 2000 (DETR, 2000a), which would be seen as high in comparison with the density in most existing suburban areas. On the other hand, there is the 100 dph, or more, found in city-centre locations. However, high density is just as much about lifestyle, physical form and sense of neighbourhood. *Intensity* is a better term because it is as much about activity, social interaction, as just a quantitative measure. It is about creating the quality of life and vitality that makes urban living desirable. Density without intensity does not work. It does not feel comfortable, just squeezed. The physical design should deal with the needs of more compact urban living.

The questions addressed at Chelmsford were as follows. What were the barriers to achieving high density? What had to be given so as to raise density? How could planning authorities place a limit on density between 'high' and 'too high'? How could they ensure that the finished product bore out the liveability advantages of high density in theory? The solution was to devise locational principles for different levels of intensity of development. An example is set out in Box 2.3. The principle should be that the intensity of new development should

---

Box 2.3   Example of locational principles for the intensity of development.

Intensity of Development

Planning permission will be granted for development, including change of use, within the urban areas and rural settlements provided:

1. The development optimises the capacity of the site. and
2. The intensity of the proposed development is compatible with the use, intensity, scale and grain of the surrounding area.

Higher-intensity development proposals will be permitted within the central area and neighbourhood policy areas where there is direct and convenient access on foot to local shops, public facilities and bus stops.

The council will assess the quantity and quality of development against the criteria set out in the accompanying tables, as well as other policies and standards in this plan.

Source: Chelmsford Borough Council.

Table 2.3 Character areas representing levels of intensity of development.

| | Higher intensity | | Lower intensity | |
	Level 1	Level 2	Level 3	Level 4
Form	Continuous frontage	Continuous frontage	Mainly continuous frontage	Landscape dominates buildings
Mix	Flats and commercial	More flats than houses	More houses than flats	Houses only
Height	Above four storeys	Up to four storeys	Up to three storeys	Up to two storeys
Parking quantity	Less than one parking space per unit	Approximately one parking space per unit	Above one parking space per unit	Above one parking space per unit
Parking design	Underground, undercroft parking, car clubs	Undercroft, decked-over parking, parking courts, car clubs	Parking squares and courts, on curtilage parking	On-plot parking
Private space	Balconies and shared garden	Balconies and shared garden	Individual and shared gardens	Individual gardens
Local open space	Urban squares	Urban squares	Parks contained by buildings	Parks with rural character
Density	Above 100 dph	40–100 dph	Above 30 dph	Less than 30 dph

Source: Chelmsford Borough Council.

reflect the existing surroundings except where high intensity can be justified, normally because of a high degree of accessibility.

It follows from this treatment of density issues that a plan should link through to more detailed physical design not just by specifying the location of more intensive development but also by giving guidance on the physical nature of the different levels of intensity that should be permitted in different locations. The first step was the identification of *character areas*, where the intensity of development was made explicit through three-dimensional physical parameters. These formed a typology that could be used to structure the locational aspects of two-dimensional spatial policy, as shown by Table 2.3. The physical implications for different levels of intensity of development for use in the development plan were made explicit by the matrix shown in Table 2.4. The *central area* was defined as land within 800 m of railway station or the town centre. *Neighbourhood* policy areas were identified within the plan.

Mix of uses

The objectives set out in Table 2.2 and Box 2.1 make it clear that the spatial policy should explicitly encourage mixed-use development. A plan should not generally zone land for single uses, but outside certain special areas, should assume a use that will be permitted if it satisfies the other policies of the plan. In the suburbs, housing will clearly predominate, but there will be other supporting uses if appropriate. Their appropriateness will be determined by the other design criteria. However, within centres, a mix of uses should be actively sought in all locations. An example of a set of policies for promoting such development is shown in Box 2.4. As with intensity, the policy should not stop there but go on to show expectations for the mix of uses in the central area, neighbourhood policy areas, the rest of the urban areas and defined settlements by means of the matrix shown by Table 2.5.

Within the general mixed-use policy areas, there will still be a need to exercise some control over the mix of type of shops in order to secure economic vitality, a proper service to the public and quality of the public realm. Clearly, though, two-dimensional land-use zoning, with areas designated for primary or secondary shopping, will not do as it cannot handle a mix of uses in three dimensions. Uses of premises above shops should be able to vary, being, say, retail, residential or office uses. A policy that controls the nature of the retail frontage to the public realm is therefore necessary. An example of the approach developed at Chelmsford is shown in Box 2.5. A distinction was made between *primary* and *support* retail frontages primarily to control the proportions of refreshment and financial services uses. The *primary* and *support* retail frontages can be shown on a proposals map by different coloured bands along the frontage of properties, while leaving the predominant notation of the map to indicate mixed-use development. The notation can be extended to show proposed, as well as existing, retail frontages.

Table 2.4 Physical implications of intensity of development.

	Central area	Neighbourhood policy areas	Rest of the urban area	Rural settlements
Quantity of development within a site, determining the intensity of development				
Density range (dph)	40–60	30–60	30–40	30–40
Minimum plot ratio	1.5:1	1.5:1	1:1	None
Height	Between 3 and 6 storeys	Between 3 and 4 storeys	Between 2 and 4 storeys	Between 2 and 3 storeys
Maximum vehicle parking	1 space per dwelling Non-residential parking varies according to type of development	1.5 spaces per dwelling Non-residential parking varies according to type of development	1 space per 1–2 bed dwelling; 2 spaces per 3 bed dwelling; 3 spaces per 4+ bed dwelling Non-residential parking varies according to type of development	1 space per 1–2 bed dwelling; 2 spaces per 3 bed dwelling; 3 spaces per 4+ bed dwellings Non-residential parking varies according to type of development
Public open space	Open space requirements can be partly met by commuted sums in lieu of provision	Open space requirements can be partly met by commuted sums in lieu of provision	47 m² per dwelling local, and 25 m² per dwelling strategic, open space. Strategic open space requirements can be met by commuted sums in lieu of provision	47 m² per dwelling local, and 25 m² per dwelling strategic, open space. Strategic open space requirements can be met by commuted sums in lieu of provision
Private amenity space (see also Box 2.9)	Exclusive private area minimum Maximum standards will apply	Exclusive private area minimum Maximum standards will apply	Minimum standards with special case exceptions	Minimum standards with special case exceptions

(Continued)

Table 2.4 (Continued)

	Central area	Neighbourhood policy areas	Rest of the urban area	Rural settlements
Quality of development within a site, determining the intensity of development				
Built form	Continuous frontage defining public realm spaces Minimal private front space	Continuous frontage defining public realm spaces Small front private space Non-residential buildings on street frontages with hidden parking and servicing	Continuous, linked or clustered frontage Small front private space Non-residential buildings on street frontages with hidden parking and servicing	Continuous, linked or clustered frontage Small front private space or garden
Public space form	Urban open spaces, such as squares and pocket parks	Urban open spaces, such as squares and pocket parks	Gardens, squares, playing fields	Greens
Private space	Gardens, patios, balconies, shared courtyards	Gardens, patios, balconies, shared courtyards	Gardens, shared courtyards	Gardens
Parking format	Underground, undercroft, rear parking courts, parking streets, parking squares	Rear parking courts, parking streets, parking squares	On-curtilage, rear parking courts, parking streets, parking squares	On-curtilage, rear parking courts, parking streets, parking squares

Source: Chelmsford Borough Council.

Box 2.4 Example of policies on mixed-use development.

Promoting Mixed-Use Development

Within the central areas within the neighbourhood policy areas, and on appropriate sites within the rural settlements, the council will encourage a mix of complementary and compatible uses in development proposals.

Within the central area and the neighbourhood policy areas the council will

1. Seek to protect existing mixed-use character and will normally refuse permission for single-use proposals replacing multiple uses or where the lack of a mix of uses would undermine the character and function of the area.
2. Seek the inclusion of non-residential accommodation in major redevelopment proposals for residential development.
3. Seek the inclusion of residential accommodation in major redevelopment proposals for non-residential development.
4. Encourage non-residential use within the ground floor frontage of proposed residential development, on streets with an existing predominantly non-residential character.
5. Permit changes of use to residential in upper floors of existing premises, except where it would result in the loss of an arts, community or leisure use.

Within the rest of the urban areas and within the rural settlements, the council will

1. Seek, in major residential developments, the inclusion of appropriate non-residential accommodation for shops, services, community facilities or workspace, located to serve the needs of the enlarged neighbourhood as a whole.
2. Permit non-residential development provided it does not prejudice the amenity, function or character of the area.

Source: Chelmsford Borough Council.

Biodiversity

The objectives set out in Table 2.2 and Box 2.1 also make it clear that the spatial policy should explicitly encourage biodiversity as a general characteristic of development and protect it on sites in addition to those with special protective designations. An example of such a policy for protecting and enhancing biodiversity devised at Chelmsford is shown in Box 2.6.

Design principles and standards

A development plan should make clear how the spatial policies find their expression in more detailed design principles. A set devised at Chelmsford is

Table 2.5 Physical expectations for mixed-use development.

		Expectations for mixed-use development in different locations		
	Central area	Neighbourhood policy areas	Rest of the urban area and rural settlements	
Location	Areas within close proximity to public transport and major public facilities	Areas within 800 m walking-distance of major public transport and central facilities	Neighbourhood centres in close proximity to local shops, community facilities and bus stops to the town centre	Areas within 800 m of a neighbourhood centre and bus routes to town centre	Areas without convenient access to local services
Typical range of activity	Mixed tenure housing Large, medium and small workplaces Major leisure/retail/hotel	Mixed tenure housing Large, medium and small workplaces Small to medium retail units Community facilities Education	Mixed tenure housing Small to medium workplaces Small to medium retail units Community facilities	Mixed tenure housing Small to medium workplaces Community facilities Education	Mixed tenure housing Community facilities Education

	1	2	3	4	5
Mixed-use form	Mainly vertical mix within schemes. Rich variety of accommodation throughout area. Virtually all ground floor accommodation non-residential	Mainly horizontal mix of workspace and residential components. Service uses concentrated at key street frontages. Close linkages between workplaces and residential	Mainly vertical mix within schemes. Virtually all ground floor accommodation non-residential	Mainly single-use employment and community facilities within residential area	Mainly single-use employment and community facilities within residential area. Industrial and warehousing units separate from residential areas
Mixed-use policy objectives	Protect existing mixed-use, especially retail, culture and leisure. Promote mixed-use in all schemes. Encourage residential in upper floors. Ground floor non-residential. Street level vitality and safety	Residential element in non-residential schemes. Non-residential element in residential schemes. Define focal locations for shops and services to serve the locality. A significant proportion of workplaces. Large developments to include community facilities	Protect mixed-use, especially local community facilities. Promote mixed-use in all schemes. Encourage residential in upper floors. Ground floor non-residential. Street level vitality and safety	Residential element in non-residential schemes. Non-residential element in residential schemes. Define focal locations for shops and services to serve the neighbourhood as a whole. Strengthen viability of the nearest neighbourhood centre. Uses compatible with residential amenity. Large developments to include new neighbourhood centre	Residential element in non-residential schemes. Non-residential element in residential schemes. Define focal locations for shops and services to serve the neighbourhood as a whole. Uses compatible with residential amenity. Large developments to include new neighbourhood centre

Source: Chelmsford Borough Council.

Box 2.5 Example of policies on retail frontages.

Primary Retail Frontages

Within the primary retail frontages and the new retail frontages defined on the proposals map, the change of use of ground floor retail units to refreshment and financial services uses will only be permitted if the town centre's balance of retail vitality and viability is not likely to be significantly harmed and if all of the following criteria are met:

1. The proportion of refreshment and financial services does not rise above 25%.
2. The number, frontage lengths and distribution of refreshment and financial services uses in the frontage do not create an over concentration of uses detracting from its established retail character.
3. The proposed use will provide a direct service to visiting members of the general public and generate sufficient morning, and afternoon and evening pedestrian activity to avoid creating an area of relative inactivity in the shopping frontages.
4. The subdivision of any unit should not create small 'token' retail units.
5. The proposal does not prejudice the effective use of upper floors retaining any existing separate access to upper floors.
6. The proposal will retain or provide a shop front with a display function and entrances that relate well to the design of the host building and to the street scene and its setting, in terms of its materials, form and proportion.

Retail Support Frontages

Within the retail support frontages and the new retail frontages defined on the proposals map, the change of use of ground floor retail units to refreshment and financial services uses will only be permitted if all the following criteria are met:

1. The proportion of refreshment and financial services units does not rise above 40%.
2. A continuous frontage of 20m or more refreshment and financial services units is not created.
3. The number, frontage lengths and distribution of refreshment and financial services uses in the frontage do not create an over concentration of uses detracting from its established character.
4. The subdivision of any unit should not create small 'token' retail units.
5. The proposal does not prejudice the effective use of upper floors retaining any existing separate access to upper floors.
6. The proposal will retain or provide a shop front with a display function and entrances that relate well to the design of the host building and to the street scene and its setting, in terms of its materials, form and proportion.

Source: Chelmsford Borough Council.

Box 2.6 Example of policies on biodiversity.

Protection of Open Land

Within the urban area, development proposals on land that has not been previously developed will be refused unless

1. The development is reasonably required and ancillary to the function of that land for its existing use.
2. It can be demonstrated that alternative and improved provision will be supplied in an appropriate location.

Protecting Biodiversity within Areas Designated as Having Nature Conservation or Other Scientific Value

The council will promote and secure the enhancement of biodiversity throughout the plan area. Within areas shown on the proposals map as important for their nature conservation or other scientific value, permission will be refused for development that would have a material adverse effect on the ecological, scientific, geological or other value of the area designated.

The weight to be attached to the harm causing adverse effect will increase with the importance of the designation. Where appropriate, conditions will be imposed or planning obligations sought to protect and enhance the nature conservation interest of the site and to provide appropriate compensatory measures and site management.

Protecting Existing Biodiversity on Non-Designated Sites

Features of nature conservation interest present on a site which has no formal designation will justify the refusal of planning permission where

1. The development will harm the features.
2. The features cannot be satisfactorily transferred to another location.

Where appropriate, conditions or planning obligations may be sought to protect and enhance the nature conservation interest of the site and to provide appropriate compensatory measures and site management.

Source: Chelmsford Borough Council.

---

set out in Box 2.7. Their overall intention should be to ensure that the development creates a sense of place, respects its context and meets functional needs. Appendices to a plan can be used to handle more detailed standards. Of particular interest here is the handling of garden size. An example from Chelmsford is set out in Table 2.6. Different approaches were set out for the central areas and the rest of the urban areas. In the central areas, as high densities were required, the scale of the provision was modest but, nevertheless, minimum levels of private open space for dwellings were required, as, for example, by provision of large balconies for flats. (A physical manifestation of this policy can be seen at Lockside Marina, described in Chapter 7, page 161.) For the rest of the urban

Box 2.7 Example of policies setting out design principles.

Designing Development to Relate to its Context

All new and extended buildings should relate to their setting to strengthen, enhance or protect local character. Planning permission will be granted provided

1. New development is well connected to and integrated with the wider settlement.
2. The siting, massing and design of proposed development makes an appropriate visual relationship with the form, grain, scale, materials and details of the surrounding area.
3. Building design is specific to the site and its context, respecting while not necessarily replicating local characteristics and consistent within its own chosen style.
4. Proposed development on sites with a high public visibility enhances the image and perception of the area.
5. Development proposals meet relevant design area objectives set out in Supplementary Planning Guidance.

Creating Successful New Places

Development proposals containing one or more new buildings should be designed to create a successful living and working environment and high quality public spaces. Planning permission will be granted provided

1. Building blocks, routes and spaces are clearly inter-related.
2. All functions are integrated into the physical form.
3. The development layout shows the way for pedestrians to move through without obstruction.
4. Public spaces are clearly distinguished from private areas.
5. Individual buildings are seen as part of a group creating a sense of enclosure.
6. Building frontages define streets, squares and green spaces; whether reinforcing an existing space or forming a wholly new space.
7. Building fronts are active with entrances and windows next to public streets and spaces.
8. Vehicle parking and servicing are placed away from street fronts.
9. Outdoor spaces are usable, safe and pleasant.
10. Threats of crime, insecurity or neglect are designed out.
11. Adverse micro-climate effects are avoided.

Existing Site Features

All development proposals must take account of the physical circumstances of the site and its edges. Planning permission will be granted provided

1. The layout of buildings and spaces within the site addresses the constraints and opportunities of the site and its boundary conditions.
2. Existing site features of natural, functional, historic or local character value, existing routes through the site and views in and out are retained and incorporated into a development proposal where there will be a public or environmental benefit to the local area.

Siting of Development to Meet Functional Needs

Proposed development should be sited to ensure that

1. Access to the site is practicable.
2. Circulation within the site and location of entrances are planned to reflect the following modal hierarchy: (i) pedestrians, (ii) people with mobility impairment, (iii) cyclists, (iv) public transport users, (v) powered two-wheelers, (vi) commercial business users, (vii) car-borne shoppers and visitors, (viii) car-borne commuters.
3. Outdoor needs are properly accommodated, including private amenity space, refuse storage, vehicle servicing and parking.
4. Buildings are orientated for satisfactory light, outlook, and privacy.
5. The use or amenity of other properties is safeguarded.

Landscape Design

The council will require that all outdoor spaces are landscape designed as an integral part of a development proposal to enhance the function and character of the spaces and help integrate the development into its surroundings. Planning permission will be granted provided

1. The landscape design relates to the function and character of the spaces and surrounding buildings.
2. Existing trees, shrubs, hedges and water features of landscape value are incorporated alongside new planting.
3. Buildings and paved surfaces are located at a sufficient distance from existing trees and hedges to avoid damage to roots from sub-surface works.
4. Boundary treatments are designed as an integral part of the development.
5. Paving and street furniture are designed for ease of pedestrian and cycle mobility, pedestrian safety and an uncluttered appearance.

Proposed new planting must be properly established and maintained in the long term. Planning conditions will prohibit the start of development until a maintenance and management schedule for new planting is agreed.

High Buildings

Planning permission will be granted for buildings higher than the existing surrounding development, unless the proposed building

1. Is in an unsuitable location for higher intensity development.
2. Interrupts an existing long-range view with specific landscape or built interest.
3. Would harm the scale of a townscape.
4. Is poorly sited in relation to the surrounding pattern of buildings and spaces.
5. Is disproportionately broad or bulky in relation to its height.
6. Lacks human scale and active frontages at ground level.
7. Has an unsightly skyline.
8. Would create an adverse micro-climate.
9. Provides insufficient ancillary space and facilities to support the development.

(Continued)

Box 2.7 Continued

Garden Size and Privacy

All new dwellings will be required to have a high degree of privacy and the use of private garden space appropriate for the type of dwelling and its location. The council will grant permission for development provided it complies with its garden size and privacy criteria.

Design of Large Floorspace Non-Residential Uses

Large-scale commercial developments must be designed to contribute to the character and identity of the area. Planning permission will be granted provided

1. The siting and design of a structure takes proper account of site features and context.
2. Building forms directly relate to streets and spaces.
3. Car parks and service bays are placed away from the street and landscape designed in relation to the building.
4. Building mass and long roof lines are scaled down.
5. Entrances, public areas, office accommodation and focal features are provided on key elevations and corners.
6. Materials, colours and signs are designed at the same time as the building form.

Design Statements

For large, complex or sensitive sites, the council will require the submission of an urban design statement containing

1. Evidence of a site and context appraisal.
2. Identification of constraints and opportunities.
3. Design objectives.
4. Consideration of urban design options.
5. The rationale behind the approach to siting and massing.
6. An explanation of proposed elevational and spatial treatments.

Source: Chelmsford Borough Council.

areas, where development was not to be so intensive, proper gardens for houses were required.

The setting out of a council's design principles in its development plan can be reinforced by the adoption of a design guide as planning policy, a process described in the following chapter. In Chelmsford's case, the *Essex guide* (EPOA, 1997), discussed fully in Chapter 3, page 47, did not just cover standards and stylistic matters dealt explicitly with general design principles.

Other policies on physical form

Policies within a development plan should empower a council to specify the mix of sizes of dwellings and regulated the design of extensions to houses.

Table 2.6 Example of garden size criteria.

	Central area and neighbourhood policy areas	**Rest of the urban area and rural settlements**
Houses with gardens	Minimum garden size will be dictated by privacy and outlook criteria Maximum size: equal to dwelling floorspace All gardens must include a private zone minimum 10 m²	Minimum size: equal to dwelling floorspace, except for detached houses: minimum size 125 m² All gardens must include a private zone minimum 10 m²
Houses sharing garden space	A private zone minimum 10 m² plus minimum 25 m² per house shared garden	
Ground floor flats and maisonettes	Ground level private zone minimum 10 m², plus use of a shared private space minimum size 200 m²	Minimum garden area: equal to dwelling floorspace Ground level gardens must include a private zone minimum 10 m²
Upper storey flats	Use a shared private space minimum size 200 m², and/or a balcony at least 3 m²	Minimum area: equal to dwelling floorspace for each flat, either as dedicated garden, or within a shared garden, minus the size of a balcony multiplied by two
Special cases	Where houses adjoin a substantial area of public open space, the accessibility of public open space combined with the better outlook will justify less private space Where flats adjoin a substantial area of public open space, accessible public open space can take the place of communal space Where buildings perform a clear beneficial role in the layout design, or where infill development restores urban form, gardens may need to be smaller or bigger to fulfil that role In physically constrained sites where development is desirable in the public interest, the achievement of a safe, attractive public realm will take priority over garden size Live–work units – the garden area should equate to the residential floorspace but the external area may be dual use, perhaps for loading or storage for the commercial element, controlled by planning condition Sheltered and special needed housing – the quality of private space will be assessed with regard to the needs of the occupiers	

Source: Chelmsford Borough Council.

Examples are set out in Boxes 2.8 and 2.9. Sporadic and ad hoc back-land development should be controlled and only permitted where a comprehensive design solution can be achieved. An example devised at Chelmsford is shown in Box 2.10.

The integration of affordable housing

One topic where published policy can be very useful in practice is for the provision and integration of affordable housing.

> **Box 2.8** Example of policy on mix of dwelling types.
>
> **Dwelling Mix**
> On development sites of 0.3 ha or more, or sites capable of accommodating 10 or more dwellings, a mix of dwelling sizes and types will be required, taking into account local circumstances and site characteristics. Exceptions may be made for development of sheltered or supported housing and housing in the central area.
>
> Source: Chelmsford Borough Council.

> **Box 2.9** Example of policy on extensions to dwellings.
>
> **Extensions to Dwellings**
> Planning permission will be granted for the extension of an existing dwelling provided
>
> 1. The roof form reflects or complements the roof form of the existing dwelling and the doors, windows and other detailing reflect the style, size, proportion and rhythm of the existing dwelling.
> 2. It does not lead to insufficient amenity space being available for the occupiers of the dwelling.
> 3. It does not result in an extended property which has insufficient off-street parking.
> 4. It is in keeping with the scale and character of the host building in the street scene generally.
> 5. It does not prejudice the amenities enjoyed by owners of adjoining residential properties.
>
> Outside the urban area and rural settlements, in addition to these criteria, extensions will only be permitted provided
>
> 1. The property to be extended is substantially intact and has a reasonable remaining life.
> 2. The proposal is well-related and proportionate to the original dwelling.
> 3. It is not visually intrusive on the skyline or in the open character of the surrounding countryside.
> 4. It retains sufficient space around the extended building to protect its setting and the amenity and character of the countryside.
>
> *Source*: Chelmsford Borough Council.

From the 1920s to the 1970s, it was common for developed countries to provide publicly funded housing for rent to those on lower incomes. In Britain, this took the form of estates, often very large ones, constructed and managed by the local council. From the 1980s onwards, the policy changed to providing subsidised rented accommodation managed by independent housing

> **Box 2.10** Example of policy on back-land development.
>
> **Backland Development**
> Proposals for new residential development within the curtilage of an existing dwelling will be refused unless:
>
> 1. The proposal contains adequate arrangements for access and appropriate parking for the existing and proposed development.
> 2. Adequate garden areas will be retained as a result of the development.
> 3. Adequate privacy is maintained between existing surrounding development and proposed dwellings and between their gardens.
> 4. There is no adverse effect upon the character and amenities of the surrounding area.
> 5. It can be demonstrated that any comprehensive development of the wider area of which it forms part will not be prejudiced.
>
> *Source*: Chelmsford Borough Council.

associations with the bulk of new provision funded as planning gain from construction of larger schemes for sale. The tenants of the council-managed estates were allowed to buy their houses. Whatever the pros and cons of the move, from the 1980s onwards one improvement was a general reduction in of the spatial separation of housing for social rent, and consequently between income groups, and the stigma associated with appearance of particular estates.

The question for current affordable housing policy was: can such physical differentiation between tenures be eliminated entirely, or at least be made to be of negligible significance? During the mid 1990s, it became clear that, left to their own devices without specific planning intervention, volume house builders would retain spatial separation within sites and physical differentiation between dwellings for different tenures. The experience of the developments considered for planning permission in Chelmsford during 1995–1996, both those described here and many other smaller schemes, was that the house builders would allocate land within the development for sale to a housing association once permission had been obtained. In these circumstances, it was in their financial interest to minimise the land area allocated to affordable housing, which was done by minimising dwelling size, garden size and parking provision, often providing the dwellings in the form of flats. In addition, they wished to place their 'finest' detached dwellings for sale on the most prominent frontage, often near main roads, relegating the affordable housing to remoter parts of the site. Unfortunately, this did not correspond to the needs of those who were seeking social rented accommodation who, within the population as a whole, tended to be larger families needing dwellings with some space, garden and a number of bedrooms. They also needed to be near main roads and public transport. Moreover, the contrast between the detached family housing provided by the house builders in that period and the appearance of the affordable housing was very conspicuous, accentuating a feeling of stigma.

The ideal situation was one in which the house builder selects a social landlord as a partner at a very early stage of the design process and where the social landlord was fully involved in negotiations and the pursuit of planning permission. The dwellings taken over by the social landlord should be the same as those being offered for sale. In other words, there should be no way of distinguishing them by their outward appearance; the only difference would be one of tenure. The social rented dwellings should be 'pepper potted' throughout the development rather than being concentrated in a single location. The integration should be 'seamless'. If the development was within a town centre, and consequently one of flats, then the affordable housing would also be flats, perhaps sheltered accommodation for the elderly or other groups with special needs. If it was, on the other hand, in a suburban estate of family houses, then the affordable housing should also be family houses.

One question that followed from this was how to respond to the increasing number of flats being constructed in the town centre, as is described in Chapter 7. A proportion of at least 25% affordable housing applied but small flats were not normally the type of dwelling that met the needs of families seeking low-cost rented accommodation. The answer was that it was not just families that were in need and, for some social groups, town-centre flats would be very suitable. One such group were the elderly. Indeed, developers were already providing increasing numbers of flats in town-centre locations for the higher-income elderly. Other groups with particular learning social difficulties, and those who had overcome their challenges and were on their way back into everyday society, could also find such locations suitable.

In Chelmsford from 1997 onwards, the policy of the Borough Plan (CBC, 1997a) required 20–25% of dwellings be affordable. Beyond this, the objectives set out earlier had to be pursued through negotiation. Some developers were more enlightened than others. The practice of selling land afterwards to the social landlord disappeared, and the social landlords were involved at an earlier stage, although often not early enough. Often the developers passed on their views, or what were believed to be their views, without the social landlord being round a table or in separate dialogue with the Borough Council. Over the years, however, progress was definitely made, and the later developments at Chancellor Park, Beaulieu Park and Great Leighs, described in Chapter 5, page 109, were achieving a standard very near to seamless integration. A standard was eventually introduced that not more than 25 socially rented dwellings, or 10% of a scheme, could be located together in any one place. An important step forward was made in 2002 with the approval by the council of supplementary planning guidance on affordable housing that set out clearly in writing all the requirements described earlier. This guidance was subsequently incorporated by the Borough Council into more general guidance on planning agreements CBC, 2005a).

Chapter 3

Guides, briefs and master plans

Any planning authority has an array of tools at its disposal that can offer broad scope for positive and creative influence if used in the right way. However, progress cannot be made by relying solely on the tactical use of procedures, permissions and agreements. They can only be successful when set in the context of design guides and site-specific guidance. This aspect of design control is of prime importance as it is the means by which all relevant aspects of a planning authority's policy are conveyed to a potential developer at the time when planning permission is sought. They enable all parties to know in advance what is expected of them and what the intentions of others are. The incremental nature of the development control process creates uncertainty. The purpose of plans, policies and guidance is to deal with this uncertainty.

The experience at Chelmsford, as set out in Part Two of this book, was that, in the event, developers, and potential developers, reacted very positively to proposals at this level of detail. Their position was that if the council had a view then they wanted to know it as clearly, and as far in advance, as possible.

A planning authority can produce a wide range of different types of planning guidance to suit a variety of circumstances. These types can include

- *Design guide* – guidance on generic aspects of urban design that apply across broad areas, such as residential neighbourhoods, throughout a planning authority.
- *Area strategy* – a long-term strategy for change for a wider area, such as an urban quarter or series of linked development sites, which paves the way for infrastructure, development and improvement projects.
- *Urban design framework* – an integrated design approach to a number of related sites and public spaces.
- *Master plan* – a definite structure of routes, building blocks, spaces and uses for a large development area, often with an implementation programme.
- *Planning brief* (sometimes called a *design* or *development brief*) – guidance for the development of a specific site containing detailed guidance on land use, access and urban design and planning obligation requirements.

- *Concept statement* – a short statement of the preferred layout and design approach to a site, produced quickly the pending approval of documents with more formal status.
- *Character appraisal* – a definition of the special architectural and historic interest of an area providing the basis for more detailed advice on design guidance and enhancement proposals.
- *Village design statement* – a description of the positive and negative elements of a village produced as a snapshot by a local community, which may ultimately be adopted by the planning authority and used in the consideration of planning applications affecting the village.

Design guides

The purpose of a design guide is to give assistance to developers, and prospective developers, through practical illustration of how policies could be fulfilled, and quality development realised, independent of site-specific considerations. During the 1970s and 1980s in Britain, the original version of the *Essex guide* (ECC, 1973) was possibly the only comprehensive guide for residential development. Other such guides that were produced had limited coverage, normally shopfronts or house extensions (Hall, 1996, 13). The situation improved enormously in the late 1990s, when many British planning authorities began producing their own comprehensive guides. Wherever they were produced, what was remarkable was the high degree of commonality of content, reflecting the progress in urban design thinking from the late 1980s onwards.

The 1973 *Essex design guide*

By virtue of its location, the guides that influenced the situation in Chelmsford were, naturally, those for the County of Essex. The original Essex County Council's *Design Guide for Residential Areas* (ECC, 1973) had been a ground-breaking document inasmuch as the content had not been set out before so clearly and as public policy. It was comprehensive, being a guide that covered all aspects of residential layout. In the early 1970s, its authors had become concerned at the poor quality of the standard suburban housing being built for sale by volume house builders, although their prescriptions could equally have applied to much of the council housing of the period. This type of development lacked any sense of place, being 'anywhere housing' that did not reflect local character. Excessive amount of space was devoted to roads and footways and was both un-aesthetic and inefficient.

The guide showed how more efficient layouts with higher densities could be achieved in urban settings but with enhanced space at the rear of the property. Such layouts could enclose space more efficiently and use traditional forms and materials to evoke a local character, in this case the Essex vernacular. On the other hand, it also argued that low-density layouts should really be low density with planting, especially trees, used to enclose space. In other words, new housing should either be at low density, with space contained by landscaping, or at medium and higher density, with space contained by buildings and being explicitly urban in form. It held that 'unsatisfactory suburbia' fell between these two positions.

Although drawn up by Essex County Council and used largely within Essex, the guide could just as easily be have been adopted by any planning authority in the country. Although the illustrations depicted the Essex vernacular style, and advice was given on it, the overwhelming bulk of the content covered fundamental urban design principles that were applicable anywhere. One of these principles was that style should reflect local character and offer a distinct sense of place. This principle could apply to any locality. Moreover, adoption of a distinct contemporary style could also be pursued without conflict with the other precepts of the guide.

The real political achievement was to get the support of the highway engineers. This involved agreement to reduction of the amount of footway and carriageway space in front of dwellings, to reflect the actual amount of movement and the use of shared surfaces. This approach was consolidated and expanded in a separate publication, the Highway standard supplement to the design guide (ECC, 1980). Unfortunately, the highways policy also contained what was to prove the principal problem with the precepts of the guide, and one where there was to be a major change when the guide was ultimately revised. This was the control of traffic through the use of extended cul-de-sac arrangements and an elaborate road hierarchy. Furthermore, segregated footpath networks separate from the road and block structures were recommended. It has to be understood that, in this period, traffic calming had not been invented as an integrated concept and such techniques would have been illegal even if it had. In the period following the publication of *Traffic in Towns* (MoT, 1963) known as the Buchanan report, the received wisdom was that the only way of obtaining both vehicle access and a reasonable standard of environment was by the separation of traffic routes from other uses.

The 1997 *Essex design guide*

The revised *Essex design guide* (EPOA, 1997) was a comprehensive text of 117 pages, and space does not allow discussion of all of its recommendations here. What follows is a summary of the principal changes from the original version.

The revised guide differed from the 1973 version in two significant ways. The complete turnabout was in road layouts. Extended cul-de-sac systems were no longer acceptable, and grid structures, reflecting perimeter block forms, were now the policy. By 1997, not only had there been substantial changes in urban design thinking on this matter, but traffic calming was legal, popular and in increasing use. The guide recommended a subtle use of such techniques to control vehicle speeds naturally. Visitor parking could be accommodated within parking courts using shared surfaces. More importantly, grids of permeable and legible streets could be created, thus facilitating the creation of character spaces and the maintenance of the urban grain.

The other difference was more a matter of greater emphasis and tightening up. What the revised guide did was to reinforce the distinction between low-density form, where space was contained by planting, and that at medium and higher densities, where space was contained by buildings and which was explicitly urban in form. For the lowest-density range, less than 8 dph, the picturesque landscape design with houses appearing at intervals from between the trees, termed *arcadia* in the guide, was recommended. For densities between 8 and 13 dph, a more formal approach with avenues of trees but still landscape dominated was recommended. For densities in the range 13–20 dph, a form termed *boulevard planning*, where space was enclosed by a combination of trees and buildings, was proposed.

The most significant tightening up was proposed for schemes with densities in excess of 20 dph. These had to be urban with space enclosed by buildings. This urban form was to have

- continuous frontage;
- building on, or near, the footway;
- modest front-to-front distances;
- shallow-plan dwellings;
- good size and shape for the back gardens.

Vehicle storage was to be behind the frontage, and within the curtilage, as shown in Figure 3.1. Proper corner types were also required. As most residential development at the time in Essex was around 25 dph, this brought all of it within the 'urban' definition. It therefore required terraced housing in most schemes and the elimination the detached houses separated only by, say, 1.5 m. An example from the guide of the recommended form for an urban street is shown in Figure 3.2.

An issue that arose in the implementation of the guide was how much semi-private space to allow in front of the dwelling. Although the guide generally showed, and appeared to advocate, none at all, there are important urban design arguments for allowing space for personalisation and other practical functions, such as refuse bin storage (Hall, 2006). The examples described in Chapters 4 and 5 generally incorporate very shallow front gardens, with decorative planting, separated from the public realm by low railings, although parts of some of the schemes do, indeed, have the houses directly fronting the footway or shared surface.

Site-specific guidance

For all the site-specific types of guidance, standard planning methodology provides, fortunately, a commonality of approach to structure. They should normally contain:

- a review of the purpose, status and setting of the guidance;
- a site appraisal;
- the policy context including relevant aspects of statutory plans and supplementary guidance;
- the design principles to be applied to the particular site.

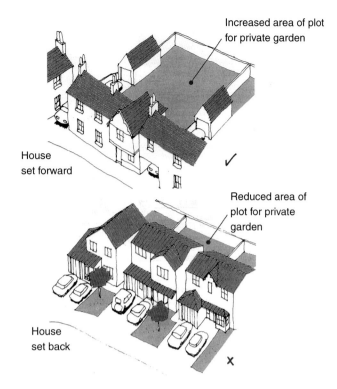

Increased area of plot
for private garden

House
set forward ✓

Reduced area of
plot for private
garden

House
set back ✗

Figure 3.1 *Essex design guide* (EPOA, 1997) – recommended dwelling arrangement for layouts at densities over 20 dph. *Source:* Essex County Council.

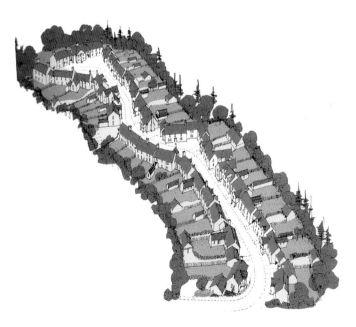

Figure 3.2 *Essex design guide* (EPOA, 1997) – case study for an urban street at over 20 dph. *Source:* Essex County Council.

What is required, in addition, for a proactive approach is for frameworks, master plans and planning briefs to include

- diagrams of the desired physical structure, blocks, frontages, access and uses;
- guidance on issues relating to implementation.

In Chelmsford's case, the distinctive aspect was the lengths the council went to address the physical structure of the desired development in its site-specific guidance. Perimeter blocks, active frontages and location of open space were all normally shown in outline. The reason for the inclusion of details of block structure with frontages was that there was, in reality, little room for manoeuvre if all contemporary design principles were to be correctly followed. Perimeter blocks tended to have certain standard sizes with limited variation. The constraints on most sites were such that there was often only one, perhaps two, ways of fitting them in, if proper frontages were to be maintained. Once the local open-space requirements had also been calculated, both in terms of quantity and necessary dimensions for particular recreational activities, the options were further limited. In these circumstances, it saved a great deal of time and trouble if the limited options were conveyed to potential developers in advance.

Area strategies

This term can be used for a document that sets out design principles for an area where there will subsequently be a complete set of detailed briefs prepared. An example is the *Chelmer Waterside Strategy* (CBC, 2002c), described in Chapter 7, page 161. This covered a very large area of brownfield land straddling a river and canal basin and adjoining the town centre. The area was divided into nine sub-areas each the subject of a subsequent detailed planning brief.

Frameworks and master plans

These terms cover site-specific guidance for large and complex areas. There are no set definitions and there can be considerable overlap between them. At Chelmsford, the *frameworks* and *master plans* covered those areas that could be developed in different segments at different times but which might not necessarily merit separate sub-briefs. They differed from *area strategies* by going into considerable physical detail and covering aspects of implementation.

An example of a largely residential master plan was that for the urban extension to the village of Great Leighs (CBC, 2001b) described in Chapter 5, page 109. An example of master plan covering the regeneration of a very complex part of a town centre was that for the West End (CBC, 2000a) described in Chapter 6, page 143. The latter resulted from an extensive public consultation exercise involving all the major stakeholders. It recommended, amongst many other things, enhanced cultural objectives and a reordering of public space and routes within the area.

An example of a *design framework* was the guidance provided for land to the east of the High Street (CBC, 2002a). This land had been viewed in the 1991–2001 Borough Plan (CBC, 1997a) as an opportunity for the expansion of large-scale retailing and multi-storey car parks together with additional open space. This development never took place and, by 2000, planning thinking had moved on. Multi-storey car parks were no longer being promoted and the attitude to retailing and open space was much finer grain. A new planning brief was prepared that set out an intricate pattern of blocks that would connect the existing shopping centre with an opened-up river bank via pedestrian routes with active frontages. Figure 3.3 shows the development framework. Note the requirements for access and for retail and other uses. Figure 3.4 shows a layout plan indicating the block structure with use classes. Figure 3.5 shows the same turned into an axonometric sketch to indicate height and bulk in three dimensions.

Planning briefs

The term *planning brief* can be used as guidance for smaller sites where development can be expected in the near future. As explained earlier, a proactive approach would require them to provide detailed guidance on the structure of blocks and spaces. Although examples of the use of this type of brief can be found throughout Part Two of this book, two particular examples are described here.

One example of a Chelmsford planning brief, that for the redevelopment of a Council depot off Baddow Road (CBC, 2003a), illustrates the handling of a small but difficult site. The site was back land with access to two main roads and was surrounded by a complex pattern of other low-intensity backland uses. Figure 3.6 shows the layout principles. Note the handling of the possible incorporation of adjacent land into the redevelopment. Figure 3.7 shows how the brief suggested two alternative illustrative layouts for blocks and open space.

An example of a brief for town-centre housing was that for the redevelopment of the former Nigel Grogan car showrooms site. Close to the town centre and public transport links, the site fronted a busy urban road, Parkway, with diverse character. It lay on periphery of residential neighbourhood and was judged suitable for urban intensification in accordance with both council and central government policy. The issues were those of scale, impact on neighbours, open-space provision, parking, building form and detailing. The planning brief (CBC, 2003b) provided guidance on land uses, site planning arrangements and the scale of buildings. The layout principles are shown by Figure 3.8. Note that the exact location and active frontage of the block was indicated together with private open space and location of trees. Indicative building height, varying with direction of frontage, was also shown. Not only was detailed advice given on the efficient incorporation of car parking in to the development, but four alternatives were proffered, as shown in Figure 3.9.

At Chelmsford, all planning briefs normally received political approval so as to give them the legal status of supplementary planning guidance.

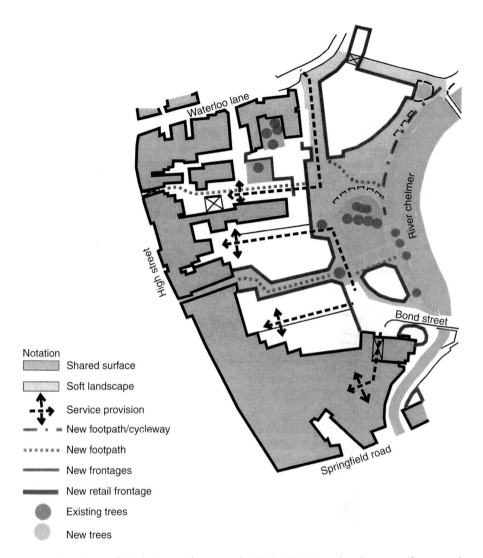

Notation

▨	Shared surface
▨	Soft landscape
⬍⬌	Service provision
─ · ─	New footpath/cycleway
∙∙∙∙∙	New footpath
━━	New frontages
▬▬	New retail frontage
●	Existing trees
●	New trees

Figure 3.3 East of High Street framework (CBC, 2002a) – development framework diagram. See also Plate 3.1. Reproduced with the permission of Chelmsford Borough Council and the Ordnance Survey on behalf of HMSO. © Crown copyright 2007. All rights reserved. Licence number 100046642.

If development came forward at unexpectedly short notice then a *concept statement*, prepared by planning officer in advance of political approval, was used. The presence of a very substantial background of general policy and guidance made this a relatively safe procedure. An example of the use of a concept statement was the development called Telford Grange, described in Chapter 5, page 105. If time and circumstances permitted, the concept statement could be converted into a fully fledged planning brief.

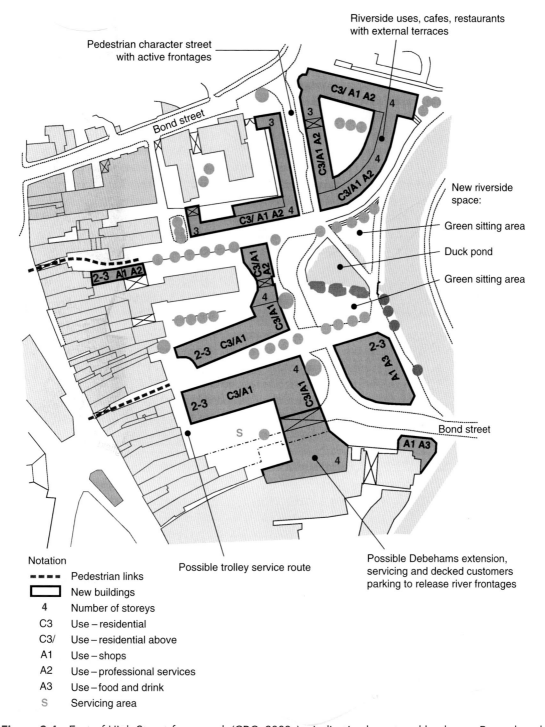

Pedestrian character street
with active frontages

Riverside uses, cafes, restaurants
with external terraces

Bond street

New riverside
space:

Green sitting area

Duck pond

Green sitting area

Bond street

Notation

----   Pedestrian links

☐   New buildings

4   Number of storeys

C3   Use – residential

C3/   Use – residential above

A1   Use – shops

A2   Use – professional services

A3   Use – food and drink

S   Servicing area

Possible trolley service route

Possible Debehams extension,
servicing and decked customers
parking to release river frontages

Figure 3.4 East of High Street framework (CBC, 2002a) – indicative layout and land uses. Reproduced with the permission of Chelmsford Borough Council and the Ordnance Survey on behalf of HMSO. © Crown copyright 2007. All rights reserved. Licence number 100046642.

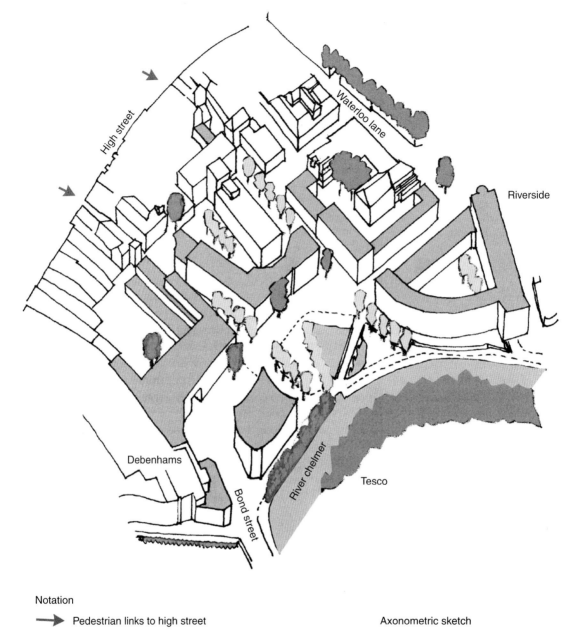

Notation

→ Pedestrian links to high street

Axonometric sketch

Figure 3.5 East of High Street framework (CBC, 2002a) – axonometric sketch. Reproduced with the permission of Chelmsford Borough Council and the Ordnance Survey on behalf of HMSO. © Crown copyright 2007. All rights reserved. Licence number 100046642.

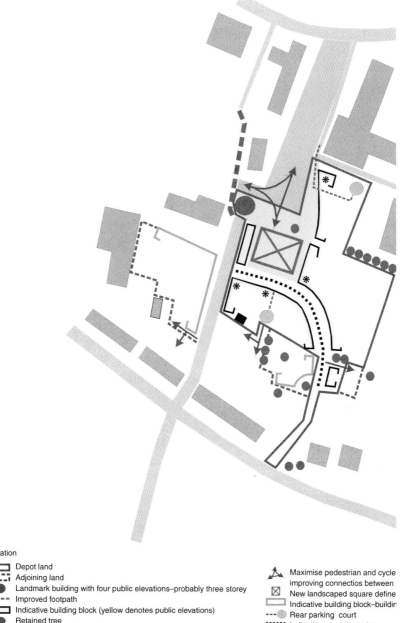

Notation

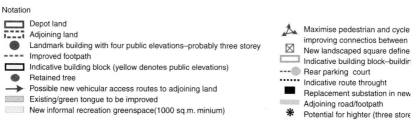

Depot land
Adjoining land
Landmark building with four public elevations–probably three storey
Improved footpath
Indicative building block (yellow denotes public elevations)
Retained tree
Possible new vehicular access routes to adjoining land
Existing/green tongue to be improved
New informal recreation greenspace(1000 sq.m. minium)

Maximise pedestrian and cycle
improving connectios between
New landscaped square define
Indicative building block–buildin
Rear parking court
Indicative route throught
Replacement substation in new
Adjoining road/footpath
Potential for highter (three store

Figure 3.6 Baddow Road Depot site brief (CBC, 2003a) – layout principles. See also Plate 3.2. Reproduced with the permission of Chelmsford Borough Council and the Ordnance Survey on behalf of HMSO. © Crown copyright 2007. All rights reserved. Licence number 100046642.

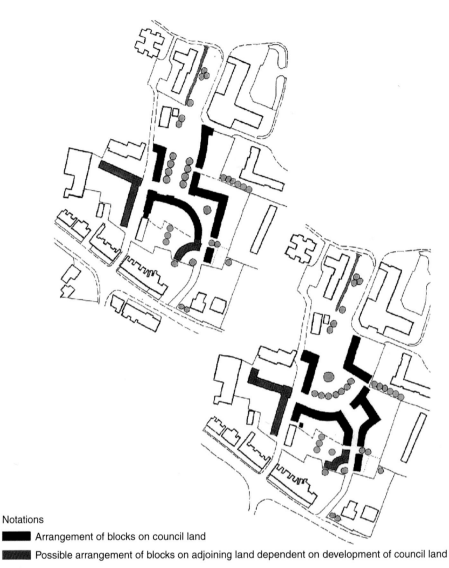

Notations

███ Arrangement of blocks on council land

▓▓▓ Possible arrangement of blocks on adjoining land dependent on development of council land

Figure 3.7 Baddow Road Depot site brief (CBC, 2003a) – illustrative block layouts. See also Plate 3.3. Reproduced with the permission of Chelmsford Borough Council and by the Ordnance Survey on behalf of HMSO. © Crown copyright 2007. All rights reserved. Licence number 100046642.

Character appraisals

Character appraisals are documents designed to guide the redevelopment of areas where there is not only to be new building but also considerable potential both for preserving and retaining existing heritage and for incorporating it to advantage in the new scheme. This is especially important where the area is not protected by conservation-area or listed-building designations and where the potential of the site may not have been previously identified.

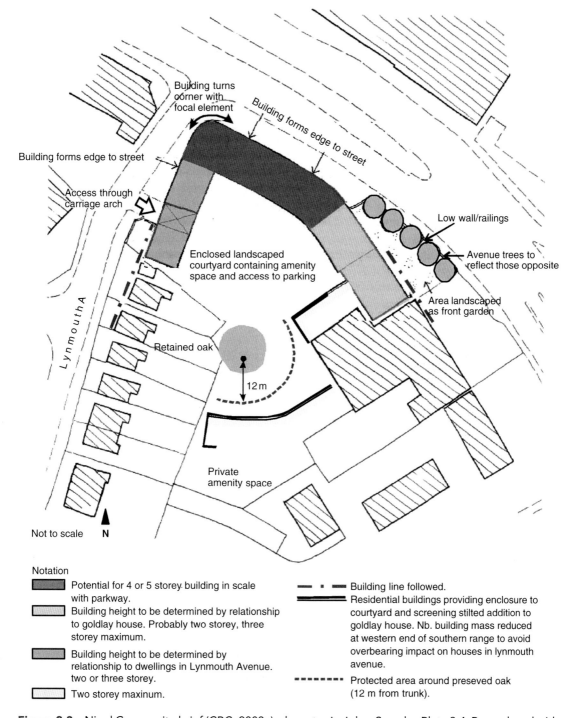

Building turns corner with focal element

Building forms edge to street

Building forms edge to street

Building forms edge to street

Access through carriage arch

Low wall/railings

Avenue trees to reflect those opposite

Enclosed landscaped courtyard containing amenity space and access to parking

Area landscaped as front garden

L y n m o u t h A

Retained oak

12 m

Private amenity space

Not to scale   N

Notation

◼ Potential for 4 or 5 storey building in scale with parkway.

▨ Building height to be determined by relationship to goldlay house. Probably two storey, three storey maximum.

▥ Building height to be determined by relationship to dwellings in Lynmouth Avenue. two or three storey.

▢ Two storey maximun.

— · — Building line followed.

▬▬▬ Residential buildings providing enclosure to courtyard and screening stilted addition to goldlay house. Nb. building mass reduced at western end of southern range to avoid overbearing impact on houses in lynmouth avenue.

▪▪▪▪▪▪▪ Protected area around preseved oak (12 m from trunk).

Figure 3.8 Nigel Grogan site brief (CBC, 2003a) – layout principles. See also Plate 3.4. Reproduced with the permission of Chelmsford Borough Council and the Ordnance Survey on behalf of HMSO. © Crown copyright 2007. All rights reserved. Licence number 100046642.

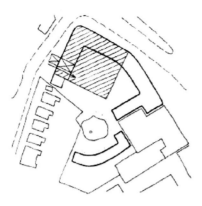

1. Potential for underground car parking, freeing up the maximum site area for private amenity
Nb. Venting must, however, be designed so as to avoid conflict with the requirement for an active frontage to parkway

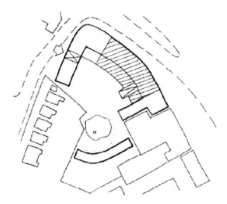

3. Potential for semi-basement/decked car parking with buildings and amenity space over

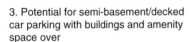

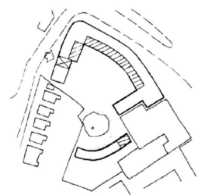

3. Potential for ground floor car parking beneath buildings. *Nb. Depth of Parkway building allows active frontage to be incorporated in front elevation*

4. Potential for car parking designed into a landscaped courtyard with high visual amenity. *Nb This option will only be supported if integrated with alternative parking solutions*

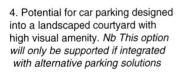

Figure 3.9 Nigel Grogan site brief (CBC, 2003a) – alternative parking arrangements. Reproduced with the permission of Chelmsford Borough Council and the Ordnance Survey on behalf of HMSO. © Crown copyright 2007. All rights reserved. Licence number 100046642.

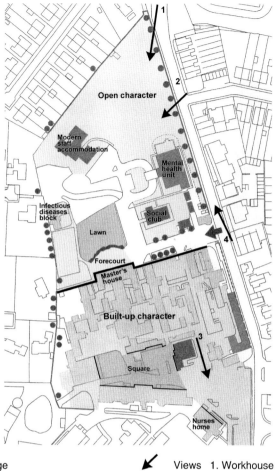

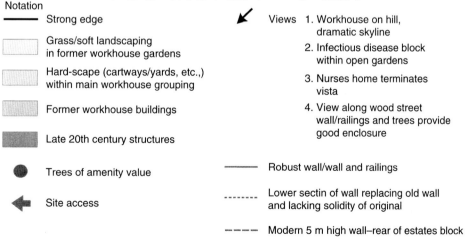

Notation

—— Strong edge

Grass/soft landscaping
in former workhouse gardens

Hard-scape (cartways/yards, etc.,)
within main workhouse grouping

Former workhouse buildings

Late 20th century structures

● Trees of amenity value

◀ Site access

↙ Views 1. Workhouse on hill,
dramatic skyline

2. Infectious disease block
within open gardens

3. Nurses home terminates
vista

4. View along wood street
wall/railings and trees provide
good enclosure

—— Robust wall/wall and railings

----- Lower sectin of wall replacing old wall
and lacking solidity of original

– – – Modern 5 m high wall–rear of estates block

Figure 3.10 St John's Hospital character appraisal (CBC, 2003c) – townscape views and spaces. See also Plate 3.5. Reproduced with the permission of Chelmsford Borough Council and the Ordnance Survey on behalf of HMSO. © Crown copyright 2007. All rights reserved. Licence number 100046642.

Indicative layout

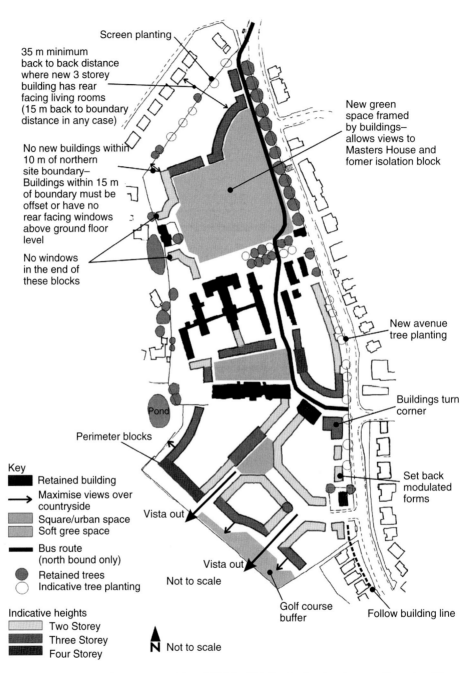

Screen planting

35 m minimum
back to back distance
where new 3 storey
building has rear
facing living rooms
(15 m back to boundary
distance in any case)

No new buildings within
10 m of northern
site boundary–
Buildings within 15 m
of boundary must be
offset or have no
rear facing windows
above ground floor
level

No windows
in the end of
these blocks

New green
space framed
by buildings–
allows views to
Masters House and
fomer isolation block

New avenue
tree planting

Buildings turn
corner

Set back
modulated
forms

Pond

Perimeter blocks

Key
■ Retained building
→ Maximise views over countryside
▨ Square/urban space
▨ Soft gree space
━ Bus route (north bound only)
● Retained trees
○ Indicative tree planting

Vista out

Vista out

Not to scale

Golf course
buffer

Follow building line

Indicative heights
▨ Two Storey
▨ Three Storey
■ Four Storey

N Not to scale

Figure 3.11 St John's Hospital brief (CBC, 2006) – indicative layout. See also Plate 3.6. Reproduced with the permission of Chelmsford Borough Council and the Ordnance Survey on behalf of HMSO. © Crown copyright 2007. All rights reserved. Licence number 100046642.

The first major character appraisal in Chelmsford (CBC, 2003c) was for the St John's Hospital site in the south-western suburbs. This site had been allocated for housing in the 1991–2001 Borough Plan (CBC, 1997a) but had, in the event, not yet been released by the Hospital Trust. The site contained buildings from different periods dating back to when it had been a 19th century workhouse. The analysis covered the origin and development, physical context, townscape characteristics and building form and character of the site. It also went on to identify both the site's negative features and its potential for improvement. At the time of the appraisal, no part of the site was protected by conservation-area or listed-building status but, on the basis of the appraisal, the northern two-thirds was designated a conservation area in the same year. An extract illustrating the analysis of townscape views and spaces is shown in Figure 3.10. The character appraisal formed the basis for a subsequent planning brief approved in 2006 (CBC, 2006). The indicative layout from this brief is shown in Figure 3.11.

Village design statements

Village design statements were first promoted in Britain by the Countryside Commission in the early 1990s (Countryside Commission, 1993, 1994). It had commissioned a number of trial studies that were successful and led to the idea being promoted nationally as standard practice. In the Chelmsford area, they were prepared by groups of people, both lay and professional, at the instigation of a parish council and with the assistance of the Rural Community Council of Essex. The scope for new development was usually limited to small scale infill and changes within conservation areas. The question of permitting, and planning for, new development and the designation of conservation areas was, of course, a matter for the Borough Council. However, once a village design statement had been completed and approved by the parish council, the parish council could invite the Borough Council to approve the document as supplementary planning guidance. Bearing this possibility in mind, the Borough Council produced a leaflet (CBC, 2000c) advising on the content of village design statements.

The first village design statement to be produced and subsequently adopted as supplementary planning guidance was for the village of Great Waltham in 2002 (CBC and Great Waltham PC, 2002). Great Waltham lies to the north of the Chelmsford urban area and has a population of approximately 2000 people. A notable feature of this particular village was that, in addition to possessing considerable historic charm and being set in a rural landscape, it also incorporated an estate of modern houses, dating from 1967 to 1971, with an unusual and innovative layout.

It is worth noting that most parishes in Essex have significant populations, some way in excess of 2000, and some are substantially urban in character. The settlements within them can be of significant size. By 2005, village design statements had been approved by the Chelmsford Council as supplementary planning guidance for five further villages.

Chapter 4

The process of negotiation

Although publishing clear policy and guidance is a necessary condition for a proactive approach it is not a sufficient one. Ongoing negotiation with developers, their professional agents and other parties is also necessary. Although time consuming, it is also rewarding if approached in a positive, constructive and creative manner and with a clear idea of what is to be achieved. It is possible, through negotiation, for planning authorities to change developers' practices. Chelmsford was able to get house builders to appoint good architects, to modify or drop standard house-types and to design new house types and one-off buildings. Through negotiation, it achieved neighbourhoods designed around public spaces, incorporating continuous frontage, buildings turning corners and hidden car parking.

In proactive design negotiations it is usually necessary to

- establish an understanding of the setting, movement network and site;
- establish a contact person, design objectives and timetable;
- insist on use of an architect;

and to end up with a site plan establishing

- shape and place of blocks in context;
- outside space – public and private realms, paths and edges;
- highway design emanating from these;
- building fronts, corners and roofs;
- building elevations and materials.

Negotiation requires time and teamwork. Checklists covering issues, objectives and design principles can be useful. Developers want a council to make its requirements clear. It is necessary to be prescriptive, to scrutinise, to challenge, to keep negotiating and to spend time on the public realm. It is necessary to encourage designers to be rigorous and ask them for design statements. Quality developers will be supportive of this process.

Stages of negotiation

Although actual negotiations can follow very complex paths, it can be helpful to use a structure based on a progressive sequence as a practical guide.

1. Understanding the site

Although it may seem a rather obvious statement to make, a good understanding of the site is essential for finding the solution that gives the best layout. For planning officers, it means spending time on site and making notes. Such analysis can become their key weapon in challenging the 'preconceived layout' approach, which some developers may adopt. Table 4.1, shows in simple diagrammatic form what a planning officer should observe, analyse and then draw lessons from when looking at the site.

For both applicants and planning officers, guidance should be offered on how to prepare an analysis of the site and its context based on linkages, setting and site features. Chelmsford published such a leaflet (CBC, 2005c) containing a checklist for carrying out a site appraisal. Its contents are shown in Box 4.1.

Table 4.1   Site checklist for planning officers.

On site and on plan	What	How
Record	What's on the site?	
What's next to the site? What's beyond the site?	Drawings with notes	
Analyse	Constraints, opportunities, influences	Site notes, maps
Identify	design objectives	Statement

Source: Chelmsford Borough Council.

Box 4.1   Advice on how to do a site and context analysis.

How to do a Site and Context Analysis

All development proposals have to take account of the unique nature of the site and its surroundings. Proposals will be shaped by site constraints as well as planning policy.

The Council encourages all applicants for planning permission to do a thorough analysis of the site and surrounding context using diagrammatic plans and sketches.

All sites are different. A sound understanding of the site itself and the area surrounding it paves the way for making the best use of land with a well-designed scheme, whether a house extension or large redevelopment scheme.

An analysis of the site within its local context will reveal the constraints and opportunities that will influence the proposed form of development.

Box 4.1 Continued

It is simplest to set out your analysis in three diagrams:

1. *Connections*
   The location of the site and its road, path and bus links with the whole town or village.
2. *Townscape*
   The buildings and landscape surrounding the site.
3. *Site Features*
   The features of the site itself and its boundaries.
   The following checklist will help you prepare these diagrams.

1. Connections

The diagram should cover an area approximately 0.5 km radius around the site.

Show	Purpose
• Main road links and where they lead to • The nearest town or neighbourhood centre • Bus stops and route numbers • Cycle ways	Indicates how accessible the site is in relation to key routes, the town centre or neighbourhood centres This will affect what kind of development is suitable
• Schools • Shops • Community and leisure facilities • Workplaces • Open spaces	Indicates the accessibility of local facilities, services and employment
• Residential districts or areas of distinctive character	Indicates whether the development site is part of a perceived neighbourhood

2. Townscape

The diagram should cover an area approximately 200m radius around the site.

Show	Purpose
• Surrounding street and block pattern • Building footprints • Building lines and skylines • Building heights • Spaces between buildings • The layout of schemes with planning permission not yet built	Indicates whether the character of the surrounding area is based on a formal or informal, urban, suburban or rural built form, and the extent to which the pattern of buildings and spaces dictates the form and layout of the new development
• Notes on age, scale, roof form, materials and typical features of local buildings	Indicates whether local building types may influence the design of new buildings
• Landmark buildings and features	Indicates the location and significance of landmarks which provide identity and orientation for the area

(Continued)

• Open spaces • Woodland • Water features	Indicates whether surrounding landscape features may influence the layout of new buildings

What you can do to help

The plan should cover the whole development site (including land in other owner-ships, or for later phases) and immediately adjoining sites.

Show	Purpose
• Topography • Adjoining property boundaries • Adjoining buildings / uses • Frontages to roads or public spaces	Indicates the falls and levels on the site Indicates the nature of adjoining private sites and public spaces which place constraints on the choice of layout of the proposed development
• Existing or pedestrian access points • Existing or potential access points • Existing paths across the site	Indicates how people and vehicles get in, out and possibly through the site at present, to help determine future access and circulation

Source: Reproduced with the permission of Chelmsford Borough Council.

2. Relating design objectives to the control process

The process of the formulation and publishing of urban design objectives was described in Chapter 2, page 24. It is important that these objectives are seen as a useful and creative tool in negotiations and not just as 'motherhood' statements or points that are taken for granted. They reduce the complexity of design theory into a collection of statements that can inform local policy. However, they still need to be translated into a form in which they can be conveniently used in the day-to-day control process.

At Chelmsford, the objectives were combined with aspects of form to see how they translated into practical considerations that could be used in design negotiations. The resulting matrix, shown in Table 4.2, was an experiment. The urban design objectives from *By Design* (DETR and CABE, 2000), set out in Table 2.1 on page 25, were listed down the left side while the cells of the matrix revealed their physical expression. When considering actual proposals, they enabled the objectives specific to the site to be formulated. When they were turned into negatives, 'the proposal does not...', they showed how urban design objectives could be expressed in reasons for refusal for use in the control process.

3. Insisting on better drawings and design statements

Obtaining proper drawings might also seem very obvious, but it is crucial. If drawings are incomplete or contradictory officers cannot rely on the quality

Table 4.2 Physical expression of objectives for design.

Objectives for Urban Design	Urban structure	Land-use locations	Layout within the site	Siting, height and massing	Safety and convenience	Appearance	Sustainability
Character	Forms coherent part of the wider pattern of development	Location of uses is right for area	Buildings form coherent group Integral landscape	Reinforces identifiable local siting, scale and form	Creates a sense of safety	Attractive composition of materials and details	
Continuity and enclosure	Continuous street frontage making streets and spaces Buildings define usable space	Allows linkage to future development of adjoining land	Clear definition of private and public areas Service area secluded	Built frontage continues existing street line Existing street form and scale reinforced	Secure boundaries between public and private areas	Elevations ordered to lead the eye and create rhythms	
Quality of the public realm	Public space is a strong component of layout Seamless link with existing public space	Public space well located Public spaces are a good size and shape	Access points and route alignments work Successful, usable outdoor spaces Ground floor uses face street	Built form reinforces existing public space	Safe, well-observed public spaces Free of clutter and hazard	Attractive and uncluttered outdoor areas Well-organised street furniture and landscape	Robust surface materials and street furniture

Ease of movement	Pedestrian routes are the basis for structure All access needs	Connects to existing network of routes Land uses and transport	Accessible and permeable layout easy to move through	Connects development to existing places and network of routes	People before traffic Movement of people creates safe place	Surfaces show routes	Easy access to public transport
Legibility	Understandable layout structure	Layout designed around vistas and landmarks	Recognisable routes, intersections and landmarks	Relates to existing views and landmarks	The layout is easy to navigate and to know where you are	Details and materials make recognisable areas Clear image	
Adaptability		Location of accommodation where it will suit different uses	Buildings Adaptable for different uses		Avoid risk of neglect and vacancy		Accommodation that will respond to changing needs and demands
Diversity		Multiple types of activity for vitality	A mix of compatible uses	Locally distinctive details			Variety of activity making a viable place

Source: Reproduced with the permission of Roger Estop.

of the built outcome. Chelmsford Council published a leaflet (CBC, 2005b) providing guidance to applicants on how to present proposals. Its contents are reproduced in Box 4.2. This also helped the planning officers assess critically the adequacy of the submitted material.

For large, complex and sensitive sites, design statements are needed to help applicants to explain their approach. With some honourable exceptions, most statements received at Chelmsford in the early days were very poor. As part of the solution, the council published notes setting out what was looked for in a design statement so as to make it genuinely useful to the planning authority. All that was required was three or four pages, illustrated by simple diagrams with notes. These had to show:

- existing features;
- limits to development;
- scope for development;
- design objectives;
- how the site layout worked;
- how siting, scale and massing relate to the area;
- reasons for its appearance;
- how the design is sustainable.

These points were included in the advice note shown in Box 4.2. Subsequently British legislation was changed to enable planning authorities to insist on the production of design statements in appropriate cases. Chelmsford subsequently introduced an online template on its web site to further assist applicants in producing the type of statement described in the advice note.

4. Analysing and challenging proposals

The first response to a drawing should be scrutiny and challenge. A planning officer does not have to be an urban designer to look hard at it and ask questions. Looking hard and asking questions is what brings out the issues. So much of the work is about looking at drawings that it can be difficult to know where to make a start in assessing them. Drawings for housing schemes, in particular, need to be analysed at many different levels. The following simple checklist can help. Do the drawings reveal the following:

- retention of existing features;
- site edges and interfaces;
- routes and spaces as key to layout;
- buildings with fronts and backs;
- buildings suiting the street type;
- seamless affordable housing;
- designed-in open space, parking, bins and cycle racks;
- public realm as an entity, particularly the treatment of surfaces?

Looking at a layout within the grain of the wider area is always very instructive. This process can be helped by reducing the layout to tracings to develop a critique.

Box 4.2 Advice on submitting clear plans and information.

The first sign of a well-designed development is a clear and well-presented planning application. A high standard of presentation is necessary to help us understand your proposal and to make a speedy decision. Drawings and information you submit with your application are used by:

- The planning application officer.
- Parish Councils.
- Neighbours and members of the public.
- Amenity groups such as resident associations.
- Technical consultants.
- Borough Councillors when they determine the application.

Your drawings and information must be comprehensive, accurate, unambiguous and relevant.

Applications will not be registered if the information is inadequate and will be returned to you for amending.

These notes set out what is needed for all applications involving new buildings, from a single house to major development layouts.

Drawings

Location Plan with a north point at no less than scale 1:1250, showing the site, the surrounding roads, paths and buildings. Ideally this should be an A4 Ordnance Survey Plan, available from your local OS agent.

Existing site layout at a scale of no less than 1:200 showing the entire property – including all existing buildings, trees, open spaces, car parking, immediately adjoining properties and boundaries.

It is most important to show adjoining properties because the grant of planning permission largely depends on the relationships to adjoining properties. Other adjoining land in the control of the applicant should be included in the existing site layout. The site area of the application should be outlined in red and controlled adjoining land outlined in blue.

Existing elevations must also be submitted

Proposed site layout at a scale of no less than 1:200 covering the same area as above, showing the siting of new buildings, vehicular/pedestrian access points, pathways, parking and servicing areas, bin stores, changes in levels, the landscape design of paved and planted areas, removed and proposed trees, the position of boundary walls and fences.

Floor plans at scale 1:50 or 1:100 for all new buildings. For extensions show the floor plan of the existing and the proposed layout, clearly indicating the proposed extension.

Roof plan showing the top of the buildings, the roof design, dormer windows, lift over-runs, mechanical plant enclosures and outside terraces

Elevations at scale 1:50 or 1:100 (consistent with floor plans). Show every elevation of each new building and all elevations affected by the proposed extension.

(Continued)

Box 4.2 Continued

In applications for an extension or alteration to an existing building, clearly distinguish existing and proposed elevations.

For all developments visible from the street, provide a front elevation showing the existing buildings on both sides. Indicate all external materials on the elevation drawing.

Site and Context Analysis

For schemes involving new development, from a single house to a major development, you should carry out an urban analysis of the site.

Your analysis of the site survey, photographs and sketches of the area should be summarised in brief notes to explain the constraints and opportunities influencing siting, scale and built form.

Please see our leaflet on How to do a Site and Context Analysis for further information.

Design Statement

For complex, sensitive or large sites the Council will require an urban design statement with the planning application to explain how the proposed design relates to the site, how it relates to its surroundings and how it helps to create a sense of place.

This should be short – 2 or 3 pages of A4 of A3, using simple diagrams of the site with notes. It should set out the following:

- Site and area diagram – noting existing features.
- Constraints – limits to development.
- Opportunities – scope for development.
- How development will integrate with the town or village and enhance character.
- How the site layout of access, buildings, spaces and parking makes the best use of the site and works well.
- How the siting, scale and massing of buildings relates well to adjoining sites.
- Why the elevations and ground surfaces will look good.
- Ways in which the design is energy efficient, long lasting, accessible to all, safe and easy to maintain.

Supporting Statement

In many cases a supporting written statement helps to provide factual background relevant to a scheme. This should be short – 1 or 2 pages of A4 only. The statement should only include information relevant to the planning determination, for example, relevant aspects of the planning history, any specific policy conflict, ownership issues, rights of way and rights to light, restrictive covenants, site contamination matters and ecological considerations.

If you feel the need to submit a more detailed supporting statement please also include a 1–2 page summary of the key points.

Supporting Statement

Urban form plan – in larger developments, an Ordnance Survey plan of the wider area can be used to show the pattern of blocks and spaces and how the proposed development fits in with it.

Axonometric and isometric views – three-dimensional views are an extremely helpful way to appreciate how the plan relates to elevations and massing. These can be simple line drawings but computer-generated three-dimensional representations are valuable

Models – very helpful to understand proposals.
Simple block models can be made from polystyrene or foam.

Perspectives – only useful if they are accurate and show new buildings in context. They are not useful if they simply glamorise a scheme.

Cross sections – useful for complex buildings or when elevations don't reveal all relevant information. A land level plan can be particularly useful if the site has significant changes in level.

Source: Reproduced with the permission of Chelmsford Borough Council.

Table 4.3 Example of urban design advice to applicants.

Urban Design Avice

Subject   **Berwick Avenue, Chelmsford   Croudace Homes sketch scheme 1538/SK9**
Date   March 2000

Issues arising from the sketch scheme. Without prejudice to the determination of a planning application.

Topic	Issue	Advice
Layout structure generally		The layout concept is satisfactory.
Public open space	The open space is under 4400 m²	Provide the amount required by the brief Show where the play equipment will go
Private garden size		Although some gardens are less than the council's standards, they are broadly acceptable in relation to the layout approach
Flat block	Height and bulk	Three storeys are acceptable if the second floor is incorporated within the roof form. The detailed form and design of this building will be critical The 19 m distance between the two wings is tight for privacy but supported on site layout grounds. Windows on these inner faces will have to be secondary and possibly angled or screened
Building line of 23	Relationship to Berwick Avenue	The house would probably be better parallel to the road, following the building line of the rest of the terrace
Existing trees and hedges	The layout needs to work around the oak trees and hedges which are the only distinctive features on the site	Show existing oak trees accurately on north and west boundaries, and hedges on east boundary

Source: Reproduced with the permission of Chelmsford Borough Council.

Another aid is blocking in all the buildings on the plan of the scheme and its surroundings to create a figure-ground diagram.

The outcome of the critique of the proposals should be an agenda for negotiating improvements. Such an agenda is found to be best set out as a personal checklist. An example is shown by Table 4.3.

5. Getting the design in context

The next stage is to advance the design by ensuring that development relates properly to the existing urban structure through an understanding of the relationships of scale and form. The context provided by an area's structure and immediate relationships is a critical determinant of site capacity. Admittedly, it is very difficult to relate development to its context without getting embroiled in matters of opinion. Nevertheless, it is important that the planning officer is able to make a reasoned case based on an understanding of the relevant context and how it should influence a particular scheme. Table 4.4 shows an attempt at this approach developed by the Chelmsford design team. Table 4.5 shows a

Table 4.4 Prompts for designing in context.

Understand the site	Topography and site features are always the starting point for design
Understand connections	How site access is planned for integration with the wider settlement
Define the relevant context for the type of development	Think carefully where to look for relevant influences – starting from existing buildings on site, to the street, to regional characteristics, to historic characteristics
Assess the sensitivity and consistency of the immediate context	The visual sensitivity and consistency of the immediate area will affect design choices Great care needed with sensitive high character areas, even if very varied in form and detail; and with areas with consistent built form or detail, even if poor quality
Identify key elements of context: • From maps • From site observation	Choose two or three key contextual elements. Use checklist of elements of context
Are elements of context essential, optional, or unimportant?	Decide how important each element of context is in relation to the particular development
Understand the site development objectives	Development objectives will affect the choice of contextual references
Is the site exceptional?	Unique circumstances may override context
Understand other visual influences:	Identify relevant historic, narrative and symbolic local references
Relate three-dimensional form to the two-dimensional site plan	Site planning goes hand-in-hand with contextual relationships
Justify design choices	Explain their contextual influences and architectural intentions

Source: Reproduced here with the permission of Roger Estop.

Table 4.5 Checklist of elements of context.

Elements of context	Relevant to proposal?	Strong Influence?	Key Points
Urban structure Network of routes Urban grain Block size Block form Street form Height to width ratios			
Spatial form Type of spaces Hard/soft landscape Space between buildings Front space Boundary walls and fences			
Built form Building line/street line Form (terrace, semi-detached, flats) Building grouping Roof form (flat, pitched, gables, hips) Corners			
Scale Storey heights Module width Roof spans Ground floor height			
Materials Palette of material Colour Texture Pattern			
Elevations Vertical or horizontal emphasis Symmetry/asymmetry Eaves/parapet line Cornice/fascia lines Window lines Elevational relief (bays, balconies, pilasters, reveals) Ground floor proportions Window size and proportions Entrance positions Porches/canopies			
Details Cills Lintels Door and window arches Decoration Glazing			

Source: Reproduced with the permission of Roger Estop.

checklist of elements of context that can be used, as appropriate, when taking forward the negotiations on a new scheme.

6. Site planning

With relationship to context established, progress can then be made on the articulation of the proposals. The process of site planning should ensure that development actually works within the site. In practical terms, this means assembling the jigsaw puzzle of buildings, spaces, uses and tenures, parking and refuse bins, and making best use of the land available. The way of organising development on the site will determine the overall density and form more than anything else. For achieving successful intensive development, this is the critical starting point

7. Making townscape

The next step is to translate the plan into three dimensions. This requires moving from plan to elevation and to a sense of continuity and space – building height, roofscape, floorscape, walls, street elevation and composition of materials. It means visualising a walk-through of the townscape and taking account of vistas, corners, containment of space and a feeling of safety for pedestrians.

During this dialogue, as the layout evolves, the urban design officers should be effectively engaged in the art of making townscape. This is a special privilege as it involves thinking about how development would look on the ground. It needs careful judgement although the process is actually very rational. Good townscape is often clearly evident from the plan but sometimes it needs more careful scrutiny. For example, it is necessary to spend time working out how gables, chimneys, dormers and windows will compose themselves. The aim should be to secure the design at this stage, leaving as little to the more negative aspects of control as possible.

8. Framing the permission

Use of conditions

In British practice, conditions attached to planning permissions are one of the most sensitive tools available for controlling the quality of design. They reinforce key aspects of the proposed scheme and help ensure that quality is carried through. Writing the conditions applied to planning consents needs care to cover the things that have been anguished over in negotiation and to realise design objectives effectively. Most design issues should be resolved before the planning permission is granted. If any aspects of design are to be reserved, it should be made clear that it is the whole design that will subsequently be assessed, not simply the technical information supplied. The hazards are that, if items are missed, then the design objective is also missed in favour of, say, a programming objective.

It is in the reasons for the conditions, rather than the conditions themselves, that the place-making objectives and aspirations are expressed. Here the language changes from the mechanical and pseudo-legal to simply explaining why. This is where the urban design objectives are really revealed. The reasons for conditions can include the topics of enclosure of space, quality of the public realm, ease of movement, permeability, legibility, character, diversity, vitality, variety, adaptability, richness, visual appropriateness and overall enjoyment.

Using informatives

In British practice, informatives are statements added to a grant of planning permission but which are not legally binding in the way that conditions attached to the permission are. There is considerable scope for influencing quality through the use of informatives. They can be used to re-state objectives and expectations. They can be used to say what is being looked for in any conditions that have been applied. A guidance drawing, or mini-brief, can often be included. It is especially useful when dealing with in outline applications where siting is a reserved matter.

9. Keeping involved after planning permission

The most dangerous time for design is the period after planning permission has been granted. This is the time when matters become very practical, and can be watered down and sub-contracted, and the vision lost. The planning officer's job is to keep tabs on this. The planner often receives a range of requests for changes, many of which need careful scrutiny. Reviewing the scheme on site as it is built, preferably with the developer, is most valuable for picking up critical aspects of detail.

Raising density through negotiation

In Chapter 2, page 28, there was discussion of how government policy requiring higher residential densities was interpreted at Chelmsford in terms of published planning policy. This policy also had to be implemented though negotiation on individual schemes. In practical terms how did Chelmsford raise the density (or, in its preferred terminology, increase the intensity) of development by negotiation? Although much could be learnt from examples elsewhere in the country, in general no such schemes were entirely satisfactory. None was entirely good or bad. Many of the well-known exemplars had special circumstances and were not typical. The answers at Chelmsford were provided through direct experience, starting with greenfield sites and then transferring the lessons learnt to very dense town sites. The results were achieved through the use of negotiation within the published policy, a process that required both flexibility and vision. What was established at the outset was that design came first; the objective to raise density came second. Although achieving higher-intensity housing inevitably required a trade-off of parking, garden size and privacy against location, design quality also meant that this was also accompanied by ingenuity in the use of layout and form. This required

Table 4.6 'Trade-offs' and 'ingenuity'.

	Trade-offs	Ingenuity
Access	Shared access	Stair or corridor
Parking	Less than 100%	Under-space, decks
Gardens	Balconies	Patios, roofs
Privacy/light	Enclosure	Orientation
Internal space	Smaller units	Internal layout

Source: Reproduced with the permission of Roger Estop.

Table 4.7 Successful and unsuccessful high-density schemes.

Yes	No
• Accessible	• Remote
• Handy shops, etc.	• No facilities
• Lively	• Dull
• Part of a place	• Out of place

Yes	No
Integrated affordable	Separate affordable
Subservient parking	Dominant parking
Lovely, useful space	Left-over space
Shared surfaces	Suburban roads
Public private definition	Public private confusion
Front or visible entrances	Back or hidden entrances
Bins inboard	Bins squeezed into gardens
Bikes inboard	Bikes under-provided
Building contains space	Objects in space
Bold (scale managed)	Apologetic (overblown suburban house)
Active ground floor	Blank ground floor

Source: Reproduced with the permission of Roger Estop.

- use of different block types – perimeter, dual aspect and vertically mixed;
- improved external spatial quality: tighter streets, efficient use of space, continuous frontage, turned corners and separate public and private space;
- vertical, instead of horizontal, distribution of uses.

Examples of what were subject to the 'trade-offs' and 'ingenuity' are shown in Table 4.6.

However, much of the day-to-day work involved dealing with a variety of small tricky sites, which were important for reaching urban intensification targets. These sites needed a context-led approach as well as ingenuity. Continuity with existing built form was the key to raising density on these infill sites. Through experience, a view emerged of what constituted successful, and unsuccessful, higher-density housing. A comparison of the characteristics between successful and unsuccessful schemes is given in Table 4.7.

A worked example

An example of the positive role of negotiation following the publication of the planning brief is provided by the case of the redevelopment in 2003 of excess industrial land at the BAe Research Laboratories at Great Baddow on the south-western edge of the Chelmsford urban area. Part of the car park, next to open countryside, had been identified for housing in an unpublished urban capacity study prepared as part of the preparatory work for the 2001–2011 Borough plan (CBC 2001a). The urban design team produced a planning brief (CBC, 2003d) that set out density, design and layout guidance based on the characteristics of the site and its setting. A particular issue was how development should relate to two existing footpaths. Figure 4.1(a) shows the suggested open-space configurations, Figure 4.1(b) the required relationship of development to the footpaths and Figure 4.1(c) gives guidance on relationship of the buildings to the main road.

The first developer to show interest in the site produced a layout that conformed to the minimum requirements of the Borough's planning policies but did not enter fully into their spirit. In particular, it did not take proper account of the content in the brief. It did, indeed, show perimeter blocks, rear parking and continuous frontage. Attempts were made to turn corners with suitable house types. Unfortunately, a rather rigid rectangular grid did not create legible and characterful spaces. This rather rigid and formal type of layout may often represent a stage in the design process but it should not be its end point. It did not integrate with the paths and did not relate well to the suburban grain and character of the area. It also showed an over-reliance on rear parking courts rather than parking within curtilage.

Building on the brief, the urban design team produced further diagrammatic advice for the prospective developers. Figure 4.2 shows the analysis of the spaces and pathways and Figure 4.3 its translation into block form. Fortunately, at this stage the site was bought by the house builders Taylor Woodrow, trading as Bryants, another house-building firm that they had acquired. They brought in Reeves Bailey, an architectural practice whose other contributions to residential design in Chelmsford are described in Chapter 5, page 95. They produced the layout, shown in Figure 4.4, which represented a full interpretation of the officer's suggested block structure. The rear parking courts in the original scheme were replaced by rear parking within curtilage as recommended by the Essex guide (EPOA, 1997). Views of the completed scheme are shown in Figures 4.5 and 4.6.

An example of the use of negotiation to produce a joint Master Plan and achieve a satisfactory layout is the case of Great Leighs (CBC, 2001b) described in Chapter 5, page 109.

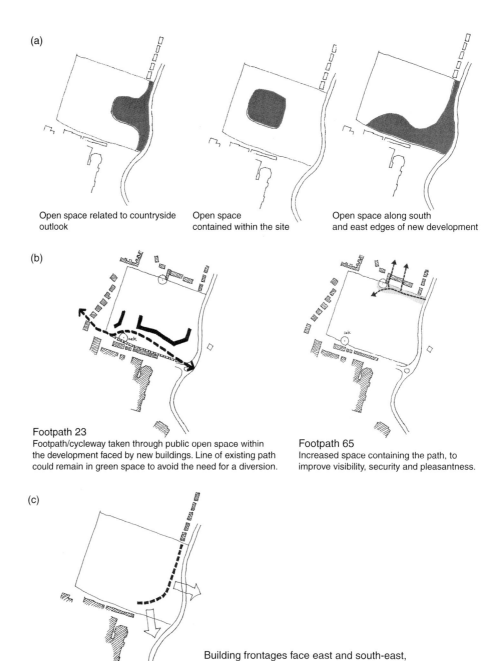

(a)

Open space related to countryside outlook

Open space contained within the site

Open space along south and east edges of new development

(b)

Footpath 23
Footpath/cycleway taken through public open space within the development faced by new buildings. Line of existing path could remain in green space to avoid the need for a diversion.

Footpath 65
Increased space containing the path, to improve visibility, security and pleasantness.

(c)

Building frontages face east and south-east, and relate to the existing building line on the north side of the site

Figure 4.1 BAe site brief (CBC, 2003d); (a) open space configuration; (b) relationship of buildings to footpaths; (c) relationship of buildings to main road. *Source:* Chelmsford Borough Council.

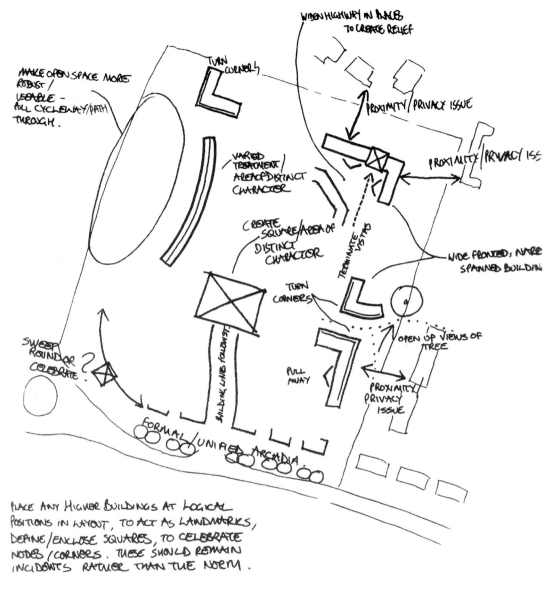

PLACE ANY HIGHER BUILDINGS AT LOGICAL
POSITIONS IN LAYOUT, TO ACT AS LANDMARKS,
DEFINE/ENCLOSE SQUARES, TO CELEBRATE
NODES/CORNERS. THESE SHOULD REMAIN
INCIDENTS RATHER THAN THE NORM.

Figure 4.2 The urban design team's townscape analysis for the BAe Site. *Source:* Chelmsford Borough Council.

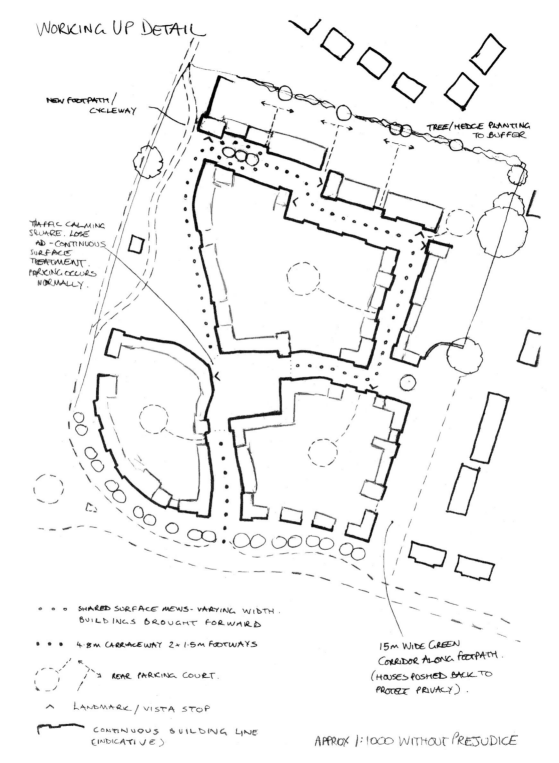

WORKING UP DETAIL

NEW FOOTPATH/
CYCLEWAY

TREE/HEDGE PLANTING
TO BUFFER

TRAFFIC CALMING
SQUARE. LOSE
AD - CONTINUOUS
SURFACE
TREATMENT.
PARKING OCCURS
NORMALLY.

• • • SHARED SURFACE MEWS- VARYING WIDTH.
BUILDINGS BROUGHT FORWARD

• • • 4.8M CARRIAGEWAY 2 × 1.5M FOOTWAYS

REAR PARKING COURT.

∧ LANDMARK / VISTA STOP

CONTINUOUS BUILDING LINE
(INDICATIVE)

15M WIDE GREEN
CORRIDOR ALONG FOOTPATH.
(HOUSES PUSHED BACK TO
PROTECT PRIVACY).

APPROX 1:1000 WITHOUT PREJUDICE

Figure 4.3   The urban design team's block structure for the BAe Site. *Source:* Chelmsford Borough Council.

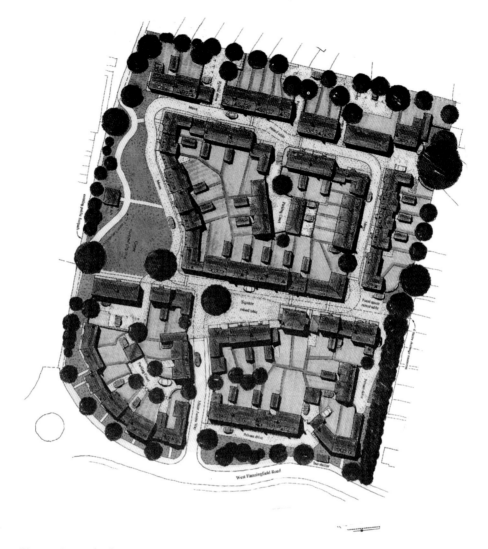

Figure 4.4 The layout produced by Reeves Bailey Architects for the BAe Site. See also Plate 4.1. *Source:* Reeves Bailey Architects.

Figure 4.5 The BAe site development approaching completion. Architecture is by Reeves Bailey. Note the provision of small front gardens. See also Plate 4.2. *Source:* Chelmsford Borough Council.

Figure 4.6 The completed BAe site development showing frontage to the local open space. *Source:* Chelmsford Borough Council.

Part Two

Origins and Outcomes

Chapter 5

Achieving residential quality

Part Two of this book describes how the quality of the built form in Chelmsford was gradually improved from 1996 to 2003. Much of the advice set out in Part One had its origins in this learning process.

The task of improving the quality of new housing built in Chelmsford was, initially, neither easy nor smooth. The 'turn around' took place over a rather dramatic 3-year period between 1996 and 1999. It occurred in three stages:

- At first, there was a period of confrontation between the Planning Committee and several volume house builders.
- Following the adoption of the revised *Essex design guide* (EPOA, 1997) in 1998, a transitional situation developed, as both planning officers and developers accustomed themselves to the changed situation.
- By mid-1999 the number of urban design officers, and the experience of the development control officers, had increased to a point where higher standards of design were becoming the norm.

From mid-2000 onwards, the situation had stabilised, providing a mature process that ensured that only developments of high quality were realised.

The period preceding the changes

Although British government policy in the 1980s had not favoured strong intervention in design matters, progress could still be made. There were some significant developments in different parts of the country, as recounted on page 5 in the introduction. Essex, in particular, had the advantage of the *Essex design guide* (ECC, 1973) as discussed on page 4. The guide had originally been produced on the assumption that county councils were the local planning authorities. However, under the re-organised system of local government that was introduced in 1974, local planning became the responsibility of district councils and the implementation of the design guide became a matter for them. Essex County Council did, however, maintain a strong design team to give advice to those District Councils unable to afford design expertise for themselves, a decision that has proved beneficial for design quality in the county over three decades.

Unfortunately, Chelmsford Borough Council had not adopted the 1973 design guide (apart from some minor elements) nor did it make regular use of the Essex County Council design team's expertise. In retrospect, this can only be seen as a missed opportunity of the first magnitude. It did not mean, however, that the guide had no influence in Chelmsford. What was remarkable about it was just how well known it became and how many architects and developers embraced it without being required to do so. Where local architects and planners believed in it, quality schemes in line with its precepts could result. Some developments were influenced to a lesser degree and a problem of superficial understanding, or even misunderstanding, of the guide began to occur, often a case of copying the pictures rather than the principles. Its influence was, consequently, patchy. By the late 1970s, when a great amount of housing was being built in Chelmsford, there were some developments that showed a high degree of influence of the guide, but others being built at the same time proceeded as though it had never existed. Unfortunately, it was that latter that predominated and some of the late 1970s schemes were truly awful.

During the 1980s, there was a lull in the rate of house building. The projects started during the late 1970s were being completed and the release of new land allocations through the development plan process had not yet taken place. Such allocations that were proposed attracted strong local opposition and the process had become mired in controversy.

By the early 1990s, the national policy framework had, however, changed decidedly for the better. New legislation had enhanced the role of local development plans and the government guidance, and planning thinking, in general, was moving towards the pursuit of higher standards of design.

The lead up to change: 1996–1997

In addition to the emergence of new planning thinking and government policy, a number of local factors came together in Chelmsford in 1996:

- a new political administration;
- the appointment of new senior staff and pursuit of a new officer and committee structure;
- the adoption of a new local plan allocating sites for a significant amount of new housing.

The process of approving the 1991–2001 Borough plan (CBC, 1997a) had been painful and long-drawn-out because of the opposition from the public to the provision of new housing. The inspector's report (CBC, 1995) had been published in 1995. It recommended the allocation of, what were seen at the time as substantial numbers of new houses to number of sites. The most significant, for the purposes of this account, were

Princes Road and Moulsham Lodge	24 ha	300 dwellings
Partridge Avenue	22 ha	200 dwellings
Beaulieu Park	35 ha	400 dwellings
Chancellor Park	37 ha	400 dwellings

The first two were predominantly 'green land' within the urban area (although Moulsham Lodge site was partly 'brownfield'). They had been accepted by the Borough Council and had been included in the draft plan. The second two were edge-of-town 'greenfield' sites, allocated by the inspector, and were highly controversial. The plan was eventually adopted early in 1997, but the first planning applications for these sites had already been made before this date. The process of preparation and consultation of the planning briefs was also well under way before 1996. For the Princes Road and Moulsham Lodge site, the landowners had engaged consultants, who had had pre-application discussions with Borough officers, before 1995.

Princes Road and Moulsham Lodge

The first planning applications for a substantial amount of new housing were from Barratt in August 1996, for the site along the north side of Princes Road, to the south of the town centre, and from Macleans in November 1997, for the Moulsham Lodge area to the south of Princes Road.

The area to be covered by the development was the subject of a planning brief (CBC, 1996a). This had been approved by the Planning Committee in October 1996 following a substantial period of public consultation, which included the landowners, their advisors and prospective developers, in line with standard practice. Compared with what to come some years alter, the brief was rather general in nature and lacked specific physical proposals beyond access points, footpath routes and the location of the principal open space. It contained a site appraisal and the summary of relevant development plan policies. However, it also contained a statement of design principles that were to apply to the site. These had been prepared by one of the Borough officers who did have urban design experience and are set out in full in Box 5.1. They were fully compatible with the contemporary urban design thinking and the principles that were to appear in the revised *Essex guide* (EPOA, 1997). The two key points were, first, the pursuit of character areas, making use of focal points and creating a sequence of urban spaces, and, second, frontage of houses to roads, including main roads.

The questions that now arose about the requirements of the brief were

Would the developer follow them?
Would the officers enforce them?
Would the committee enforce them?

The answer to the first two questions turned out to be no.

Box 5.1 Extract from the planning brief for *Land off Princes Road* (CBC, 1996a) showing the design principles employed.

11. DESIGN AND LAYOUT

Design Principles

11.1 In view of the large area and the lack of any strong pattern or character within the surrounding developments, the new housing areas should create their own strong character, pattern of development and identity.

11.2 The existing site features and constraints should be taken as the basis for the housing layout and used as opportunities to create features focal points and interest within the development.

Development Edges

11.3 A number of new development edges will occur to new and existing road frontages and to the open spaces. Public open spaces should be treated as focal points with houses fronting on to them. New and existing roads should also be fronted by houses, even when it is not possible to take direct vehicular access from a major road. In such circumstances, access can be taken from service roads or private drives running parallel or from the rear.

11.5 The layouts should avoid the rear and side gardens of existing properties from becoming frontages to new public spaces or road frontages.

Structure

11.6 Within the sites, the new development should be laid out to form a coherent network of spaces, enhanced by appropriate built form. These should be designed for the pedestrian viewpoint relating to the human scale and creating an environment which encourages cycling and walking to reach local destinations.

11.7 Visual interest and variety should be created by an unfolding sequence of spaces, varied design of buildings and open views.

Character Areas

11.9 The non-residential elements which serve the development should be grouped in an integrated manner to form a core urban space. Parking provision should not dominate this space where residential densities can also be higher. Pedestrian and cycleway routes should radiate from the core areas as well as the street network.

11.10 In addition to the core, housing should be structured around a series of nodal points. These should be irregular or regular shaped urban spaces formed at junctions of routes and emphasised by key buildings or building groups. Areas with their own identity can thus be created.

11.11 Dwelling sizes and forms should be mixed within the development so as to assist the creation of visual variety, interest and townscape.

11.12 Development should generally be of one, two or three storeys providing the opportunity to create landmarks with distinctive buildings or spaces at points where they can aid orientation and the creation of townscape.

11.13 Throughout the development, views and open spaces should be used to provide legibility and to reduce the apparent bulk of the housing provision.

Permeability

11.15 It should be possible for pedestrians and cyclists to move freely between all parts of the layout, both locally and on a wider scale. If culs-de-sac are used, their heads should be linked by creating pedestrian/cycle links between the road systems to avoid dead ends.

Detailed Design

11.16 Detailed dwelling design should avoid the following:
Vehicle dominated forecourts and drives
Deep plan dwellings in visually prominent positions
Dominant front appendages
Staggered/ sawtooth frontages.

Secured by Design

11.17 Development of the site should be discussed with the Police to ensure that the layout complies with their objectives of providing a safe and secure environment. In particular, the residential layout must ensure satisfactory surveillance of the local public open space.

Materials

11.18 The facing and roof materials should be selected from the traditional range of materials characteristic of Essex, particularly in key locations. Modern derivatives of these may be acceptable in less prominent locations.

Screen Walls and Fences

11.19 Screen walls and fences adjoining roads and public areas should be avoided.

Source: Reproduced with the permission of Chelmsford Borough Council.

There was, unfortunately, little sign of the qualities referred to in the brief in the schemes submitted by the volume house builders. Both schemes were layouts of standard house-types with little in the way of characterful urban spaces and numerous instances of lack of frontage, particularly to main roads. They were a narrow range of standard house types, usually detached with integral garage, deep-plan in form and with pseudo-vernacular decoration applied to the front only. They were set with minimal side-to-side spacing. There was road-dominated townscape, lack of enclosure of space and frequent examples of exposed sides and backs of properties. This was not as good as the best developments in Chelmsford during the late 1970s and early 1980s. It was the ubiquitous standard product that showed no evidence of the house builders having learnt from the *Essex design guide* (ECC, 1973) let alone being consistent with the contemporary ideas. The scene was set for a struggle.

The development control officers negotiated some minor improvements but did not confront the overall design failings of the schemes by recommending refusal of permission. The reasons given by the officers for their recommendations, and also for not producing more prescriptive briefs, were similar to those current during the 1980s when government policy did not support strong intervention in matters of design. In other words, they did not argue that they liked the schemes but they did not believe they could justify intervention. It is worth noting that, even as much as 10 years later, the Commission for Architecture and the Built Environment (CABE, 2006) was still needing to counter views amongst British planning officers that refusal of permission on design grounds could not be sustained on appeal.

Although both schemes were recommended by the council's officers for approval, the planning committee expressed significant reservations about them. Alterations were agreed after substantial further negotiation between the applicants and both officers and representatives of the committee, mainly in an attempt to increase the amount of frontage to roads and increase the use of terrace houses and to achieve at least some semblance of character spaces in the public realm. The Barratt scheme was reluctantly approved, as was two-thirds of the Macleans layout. One achievement on the south side of Princes Road was the provision of some degree of defined and active frontage through the use of terraced houses and small blocks of flats that could be used to turn corners. Macleans had originally wanted to use the road to display their larger detached houses. Unfortunately, no proper frontage was obtained on the northern side of the road. Views of parts of the completed schemes are shown in Figures 5.1 and 5.2.

For the remaining third of the Macleans scheme, agreement could not be reached and the issue went to appeal by public enquiry in June 1998. The author

Figure 5.1   The Princes Road development by Barratt in the late 1990s using their standard house-types. *Source:* Tony Hall.

acted as the witness for the council. The appeal was decisively dismissed by the inspector. Unfortunately, this decision was later overturned by the courts on a minor, and controversial, legal point. A new inquiry was held in 1999 and the appeal was again dismissed.

The significance of these initial events was that they demonstrated that intervention on design grounds was possible and refusal would be sustained on appeal. The disappointing aspect was that a large section of the urban area of Chelmsford had been redeveloped to a standard that, although better than originally submitted, and better than what was happening in many other parts of the country, was substantially lower than that which was to be achieved in the years that followed. At least, though, it was to be the last of its type in Chelmsford.

The initial proposals for Chancellor Park

A similar struggle occurred within with the urban extension to the north-east of the town by Taylor Woodrow that became known as Chancellor Park. The planning brief (CBC, 1997b) included the same design principles as those for Princes Road, as set out in Box 5.1. They required frontage to roads, including main roads. Notwithstanding this, a 'master plan', similar to other developer master plans of the period, was produced by Taylor Woodrow. It showed only a skeletal road network and the principal areas of public open space. It also showed where the developer thought active frontage should occur on the principal roads and, by implication, where it would not. In particular, there was no frontage to main

Figure 5.2 The Moulsham Lodge development by Macleans in the late 1990s using their standard house-types. *Source:* Tony Hall.

Figure 5.3 The first stage of the Chancellor Park development showing Taylor Woodrow's standard house-types. *Source:* Tony Hall.

traffic route bordering the scheme, as had been the practice with housing lay-outs of the late 1970s. Later in 1997, approval was sought for the 'master plan' and for an initial planning application for part of the site adjoining the main road. It had Taylor Woodrow's standard detached houses backing on to the main road. Although recommended for approval by officers, the committee refused it and further stated that the provisions of the brief would take precedence over the developer's master plan in all cases. This application, and several other layouts for other parcels of land that were already in the pipeline, were amended though negotiation to ensure proper frontage and reasonable urban spaces. They were eventually granted permission and constructed during 1998. However, they were still the standard house-types, mostly detached, as shown in Figure 5.3.

The transitional phase: 1998–1999

The next tranche of housing developments that came forward could be seen as representing a transitional phase. They represented a significant improvement on the Princes Road and Moulsham Lodge schemes but were still not wholly up to the full standards expected by the revised Essex guide (EPOA, 1997). This had been adopted by the council as supplementary planning guidance in March 1998 and introduced the strict requirement for continuous frontage in urban schemes described on page 48 in Chapter 3. The Borough Council now had similar planning briefs to that for Princes Road in place for all the new housing sites expected to be developed in the near future, both large and small. Although these briefs did not go into the physical detail, such as outlines of blocks, that was to be seen later, they did embody the essential design principles set out in Box 5.1.

Typical of this transitional stage was the site at Partridge Avenue, former playing fields in the north of the urban area, developed during 1998–1999 by a number of house-building firms and which ended up somewhat uneven in quality. One the last segments, built by Wimpey in 1999, represented the first genuine attempt to meet the objectives of the 1997 Essex guide by means of continuous frontage and use of corner types. Earlier parts of the site, developed by different firms during 1998 and 1999, were more of a compromise between the expectations of the guide and the developers' standard house-types and layouts. Nevertheless, a definite change in physical form could now be seen on the ground. It was a similar story for the smaller site of Berwick Avenue nearby, which, because of protracted negotiations, was not completed until 2001.

The initial stages of Beaulieu Park

An equivalent, possibly greater, range of negotiations and outcomes occurred in relation to, Beaulieu Park, the second major urban extension of 400 dwellings on the north-east boundary of the town. It was certainly a site where the changes in policy at local and central government levels were to played be out over a lengthy period. A planning brief (CBC, 1996b) of the more general type produced at that time for Princes Road and other sites, had also been approved for Beaulieu Park. As at Chancellor Park, the leading developers, in this case Countryside Properties, proceeded by means of their own master plan. This set out a skeletal road network, but not blocks, and the location of the principal areas of public open space. One special feature was a fairly large park, partly laid out as formal gardens. This type of park was an unusual, but very welcome, feature in a new estate. As was also to happen at Chancellor Park, a variant of the master plan partitioned the site into separate parcels of land to be developed at different times and, in some cases, sold to other developers.

Countryside Properties' original concept was characteristic of the densities employed at the time, averaging 20–25 dph with the use of large detached houses. The use of traffic calming enabled the principal estate roads to be laid out as formal boulevards without the danger of high traffic speeds. Had there not been a subsequent change of policy on residential density by both the central government and the Borough Council, the whole estate would probably have ended up very similar to Great Notley Garden Village, in Braintree, also by Countryside Properties, and Kingshill Village at West Malling in Kent.

The first stage, commenced in 1997, consisted of very large detached houses in a pseudo-classical style. Some took advantage of a specially prepared vista towards New Hall, a grade 1 listed building, or views towards the new park, as shown in Figure 5.4. The developer's argument was that these came within the landscape dominated 'boulevard' provisions of the Essex guide (EPOA, 1997), which was allowed in densities up to 20 dph. This followed the desire of house

Figure 5.4 The first stage of the Beaulieu Park development by Countryside Properties showing their detached houses fronting the new park. *Source:* Chelmsford Borough Council.

builders at the time to 'front' their schemes with what they considered to be their most impressive houses relegating smaller properties, to the rear of the site. At Beaulieu Park, such properties were, indeed, both conspicuous and expensive, but they were to be the last of their type built on this scale in Chelmsford.

The next stage, fitting in housing behind the grander avenues, came in late 1998 and proved more controversial. Although assurances had been given by Copthorne Homes, a Countryside Properties subsidiary, that this development would follow the precepts of the 1997 guide, and that the agreement of the Essex County Council design team would be sought, the first layouts presented did not so conform in the opinion of both the author and the Essex County Council design team. The problem was that the developers wanted large detached houses, in a 'New England' rather than Essex style, that was neither low-density 'boulevard' form nor 'urban' as conceived by the guide. Examples of how it might have turned out can be seen at Great Notley Garden Village, in the layouts behind the formal boulevards. Much negotiation ensued and, eventually, a compromise was reached and planning permission given. The resulting development, completed in 1999, is illustrated in Figure 5.5. However, this too was to be the last housing of its type in Chelmsford, just as those at Beaulieu Park Phase 1 and at Princes Road and Moulsham Lodge had also been the last of their types.

Figure 5.5   The second stage of the Beaulieu Park development by Copthorne. *Source:* Chelmsford Borough Council.

The New Order emerges: 1999–2000

Bishops Mead

What was to ultimately prove an even more significant and positive chain of events now began at Chancellor Park. Following the difficulties they had had with the planning committee in 1997, the developers, Taylor Woodrow, had a major change of heart. Rather than go to appeal or continue fractious negotiations, and noting the resolve of the Planning Committee, they sought a new design approach. They recalled that, at their new development at Coldharbour Way at Aylesbury, Buckinghamshire (CABE and ODPM, 2002, 54) they had employed an architect, John Simpson, who had been producing the higher quality of housing that Chelmsford Council now appeared to be demanding. His advice was sought on Chancellor Park but, unfortunately, he was not available for the work himself. Taylor Woodrow turned then to Reeves Bailey, a practice who specialised in the same style and quality of housing.

Using a range new house types designed for the site, they produced designs entirely in conformity with the Essex guide (EPOA, 1997), expressing not just its

Figure 5.6 The layout for the Bishops Mead scheme at Chancellor Park prepared by Reeves Bailey Architects for Taylor Woodrow. See also Plate 5.1. *Source:* Reeves Bailey Architects.

details but also its philosophy. Style was traditional but incorporated shallow-plan forms, parking behind buildings within curtilage, character spaces and aesthetically satisfying and legible townscape. The first parcel of land that they worked on, Bishops Mead, was given planning permission and was constructed in 1999. The plan of the layout is shown in Figure 5.6. It located new frontage on the existing main road and created character spaces as required by the brief. It employed an Essex vernacular style, with continuous frontage and rear parking arrangements, in line with the Essex guide. In doing so it achieved a density of just over 33 dph. The scheme won a Housing Design Award for 2002.* The central parking court is shown in Figure 5.7 and street scenes in Figures 5.8 and 5.9.

---

*The British housing design awards are held each year to celebrate new housing schemes that reflect not only the highest standard of architecture but also those developments that make a lasting difference to the communities they serve. They are designed to reward all the bodies responsible for good housing design, including the relevant planning authorities and funding agencies, as well as designers and developers. The awards are run jointly by the government, the National Housebuilding Council, the Royal Institute of British Architects and the Royal Town Planning Institute.

Figure 5.7 The central square and visitors parking court at Bishops Mead. Note the provision of small front gardens. *Source:* Chelmsford Borough Council.

Looking at the layout more closely, the first point to note is that the layout was conceived in terms of a sequence of public spaces. These spaces were defined by genuine continuous frontage. In many, but not all, cases, small front gardens, separated by low railings from the public realm, were provided. Wider spaces were paved and planted to accommodate visitor parking without giving the appearance of there being defined visitor parking spaces. Residents' parking was not just to the rear, but also within curtilage. The special touch was to place wooden gates across the vehicle entrances, providing not only security but also ensuring that visual continuity of frontage was not interrupted. The neovernacular design of the gates was also pleasing. The continuity of frontage was achieved by the use of specially designed house types. This included both dwelling types with right-angled corners and ones with more gradual corners using obtuse angles.

The change of heart by Taylor Woodrow was not just a matter of stylistic content and adherence to design principles but was also about ways of proceeding. Rather than employ architects, or other designers, by competitive tender, to lay out their pre-designed house types, they had employed a specialist architectural practice to design the whole scheme. The architects designed the houses themselves and laid them out not only according the design principles but also in relation to the nature of the particular site. The practice could negotiate directly with the Borough's urban design team and build up an understanding that would carry over to the consideration of future planning applications. In these circumstances, consideration by the planning committee went very smoothly.

Figure 5.8   A side street at Bishops Mead, architecture by Reeves Bailey. Note the gates that give access to the rear garages. See also Plate 5.2. *Source:* Chelmsford Borough Council.

Figure 5.9   A side street at Bishops Mead. *Source:* Tony Hall.

The properties were well received by prospective buyers and sold well. One anecdote, though, may serve to illustrate the new residents' sense of ownership of the design. After the houses in Bishops Mead had been sold, the central shared surface for visitor parking was being paved with grey asphalt rather than the advertised coloured surface. The purchasers protested that this was not the product they had paid good money for. They wanted the original design and eventually the builder had to provide a coloured surface.

The subsequent stages of Chancellor Park

Other significant parts of Chancellor Park were subsequently designed by Reeves Bailey to the same standards and constructed in 2000. Unfortunately, some other substantial sections of the Chancellor Park development had been sold off in 1999 to other volume house builders who did not operate in the manner that Taylor Woodrow were now doing. However, the appointment of more urban designers by the Borough Council was starting to make an impact. The volume house builders concerned were required to fit their house types together to form continuous frontages, to create reasonably effective public spaces and to locate private parking at the rear of the properties. However, compared with the Reeves Bailey sections, their conformity to the policies appeared reluctant, if judged by the appearance of the results. One of the issues appeared to be a reluctance to link more than two houses together in terraces if this could be avoided. Others were the quality of building materials and finishes, and the quality of landscaping and paving. In addition, the overall quality of the individual houses was not as good as what was to come later.

The intermediate stages of Beaulieu Park

After 1999, the situation at Beaulieu Park estate began to improve markedly. There was a definite change in the nature of both procedures and outcomes. The developers were now going along with the higher-density layouts, which conformed to a greater degree to both the emerging central government policy and the 'urban' scenarios of the Essex guide (EPOA, 1997). This also had the great advantage for the developers of providing significantly more dwellings than had originally been intended. Matters had, though, been made more complex by the parcelling up and selling off of most of the remaining sites to other house builders. On the Borough Council's side, the emergence of a stronger design team was now producing results from a stronger negotiating presence. As the development progressed, so the standard of layout could be seen to improve. Although there was still a preponderance of larger houses and neoclassical styles, the intermediate stages of the development, to the south and east of the site, had a greater degree of continuous frontage, densities of at least 30 dph and parking to the rear of dwellings. The paving of roads and footpaths became more informal. Figures 5.10 and 5.11 show examples of the urban form from this period.

Figure 5.10 A street scene from intermediate period of the Beaulieu Park development. In the foreground, 'boulevard' form is created by detached houses in a neoclassical style fronting an avenue of trees. This leads through to a more urban layout in a neovernacular style. *Source:* Chelmsford Borough Council.

Figure 5.11 A street scene from intermediate period of the Beaulieu Park development showing town houses in a neoclassical style. *Source:* Chelmsford Borough Council.

Writtle Road, Parkinson Drive

The development in Writtle Road to the south of the town centre, later named Parkinson Drive, could be seen as forming part not only of the story of the higher standards of residential design but also the story of higher density living in the central area as described in Chapter 7. However, the site was not really part of the town centre and was more suburban in location, in spite of its higher-density form. The site was a factory complex that had been derelict for many years. Redevelopment for housing, although pressed for by housebuilders and the owners, had not been permitted because of the Essex County Council structure plan (ECC, 1991, 1995) and *Chelmsford Borough Local Plan* (CBC, 1997a) policies that reserved such sites for industrial or office use. However, no such uses had been forthcoming and the progressive de-industrialisation of the economy had rendered it most unlikely. Eventually, central government and Chelmsford Borough polices (although not Essex County Council) moved towards seeing such sites as fit for residential or, ideally, mixed-use, redevelopment. The Borough allowed the change of use, and loss of 'employment land', on the basis that a mixed-use scheme would be produced. The delay though, was a blessing in disguise as, by the time planning permission was finally granted, policies on density and urban design had also moved forward.

As the site was close to the town centre, it was suitable for a higher-density development of flats and town houses. There were good cycle and footpath links to the centre, which was only 15-min-walk away. Most of the existing buildings were either derelict or unsuitable for conversion, but one block, fronting Writtle Road, was considered worthy of retention.

In late 1996, the site's then owners, GEC-Marconi, asked Mel Dunbar Associates to prepare a mixed-use, predominantly residential, scheme. This took the form of perimeter blocks on a rectangular street grid using town houses with flats to turn the corner and a central formal open space. Unfortunately, GEC-Marconi underwent structural changes, leading ultimately to the break-up of the company, and they put the land on the market. It was bought by Fairview, who started negotiations afresh with the council. The urban design team actively pressed for a scheme of urban character and encouraged a permeable, street-based layout using perimeter blocks.

In 2000, Fairview came up with a scheme outwardly similar to the Mel Dunbar layout but with much plainer architecture. It was one of the first housing schemes in Chelmsford to be provided with a properly worked-up design statement by the developers. A plan of the layout is shown in Figure 5.12. As with the previous scheme, the perimeter block form of the development, enclosing private space, was clearly stated and provided a setting for public space. Parking was placed in the middle of the blocks, in the private realm, instead of wide streets with frontage parking as seen in urban perimeter block schemes in some other parts of the country at that time. Legibility was good, with the straight streets providing views linking new urban spaces. It had a strong street character. The scheme worked well with the grain of the predominantly terraced existing area. The non-residential uses were business units in to the west of the site and

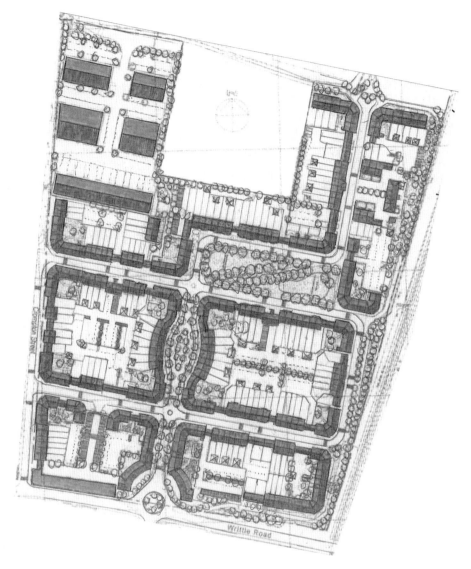

Figure 5.12 The layout for the Writtle Road, Parkinson Drive, scheme prepared by PRP Architects for Fairview. *Source:* PRP Architects.

a doctor's surgery and shops in the former factory building on the Writtle Road frontage, which was retained and converted. The scheme contained 520 dwellings, with a range of one to five bedrooms, comprising both flats and houses. The density worked out at 55 dph. A direct footpath and cycle way link to the town centre was provided. Street views of the completed scheme are shown in Figures 5.13 and 5.14.

Although, in many ways, the development represented a significant step forward, unfortunately, not all aspects of the scheme were ideal. This was

Figure 5.13 Flats used to turn corners at the centre of the Writtle Road development. *Source:* Chelmsford Borough Council.

Figure 5.14 Town houses facing a small green at the centre of the Writtle Road development. *Source:* Chelmsford Borough Council.

Chelmsford's first experience of a large-scale high-density residential scheme and the council was not yet able to secure from the developers the quality of final outcomes that were to be achieved a few year later. The perimeter blocks were large so as to accommodate not just the private open space but also some deep-plan house types and large parking courts, which was not in the spirit of the Essex guide (EPOA, 1997). Many visitors disliked the hardness of the townscape on many of the streets, and the lack of provision for personalisation and refuse bin storage on the frontages, as may be seen from Figures 5.13 and 5.15. Whereas the town houses in Figure 5.14 had shallow front gardens, separated by low railings, nearly all the rest of the flats and houses had none. The town houses in the northern part of the development had recessed porches below small balconies, as shown in Figure 5.15. Although these recesses were desirable in themselves, there was still no soft interface between building and footway and only limited scope for personalisation and bin storage. The affordable housing (not illustrated) had no such recesses and the townscape in this part of the development was especially severe.

Remarkably, it later emerged that, whatever the position of the developers, Fairview may or may not have been, the views of the architects PRP were, in reality, very close to those of the Chelmsford Borough design team. Had the architects and planning officers been allowed to work together in close partnership from the very beginning, on the lines advocated in Chapter 4, then the final shape and quality of the scheme may very well have been significantly different. Such working arrangements were established with later schemes and this experience lies behind the advice given in Part One.

Figure 5.15 Frontage details of town houses in the northern section of the Writtle Road development. *Source:* Tony Hall.

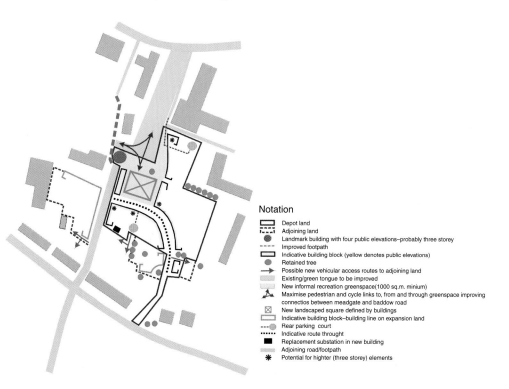

Notation

- Shared surface
- Soft landscape
- Service provision
- New footpath/cycleway
- New footpath
- New frontages
- New retail frontage
- Existing trees
- New trees

Waterloo lane

High street

River chelmer

Bond street

Springfield road

Plate 3.1 East of High Street framework (CBC, 2002a) – development framework diagram. Reproduced with the permission of Chelmsford Borough Council and the Ordnance Survey on behalf of HMSO. © Crown copyright 2007. All rights reserved. Licence number 100046642.

Notation

- Depot land
- Adjoining land
- Landmark building with four public elevations–probably three storey
- Improved footpath
- Indicative building block (yellow denotes public elevations)
- Retained tree
- Possible new vehicular access routes to adjoining land
- Existing/green tongue to be improved
- New informal recreation greenspace(1000 sq.m. minium)
- Maximise pedestrian and cycle links to, from and through greenspace improving connectios between meadgate and baddow road
- New landscaped square defined by buildings
- Indicative building block–building line on expansion land
- Rear parking court
- Indicative route throught
- Replacement substation in new building
- Adjoining road/footpath
- Potential for highter (three storey) elements

Plate 3.2 Baddow Road Depot site brief (CBC, 2003a) – layout principles. Reproduced with the permission of Chelmsford Borough Council and the Ordnance Survey on behalf of HMSO. © Crown copyright 2007. All rights reserved. Licence number 100046642.

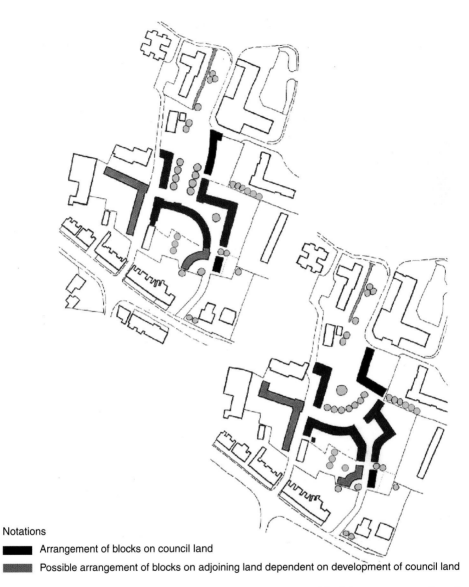

Notations

■■■ Arrangement of blocks on council land

▓▓▓ Possible arrangement of blocks on adjoining land dependent on development of council land

Plate 3.3 Baddow Road Depot site brief (CBC, 2003a) – illustrative block layouts. Reproduced with the permission of Chelmsford Borough Council and the Ordnance Survey on behalf of HMSO. © Crown copyright 2007. All rights reserved. Licence number 100046642.

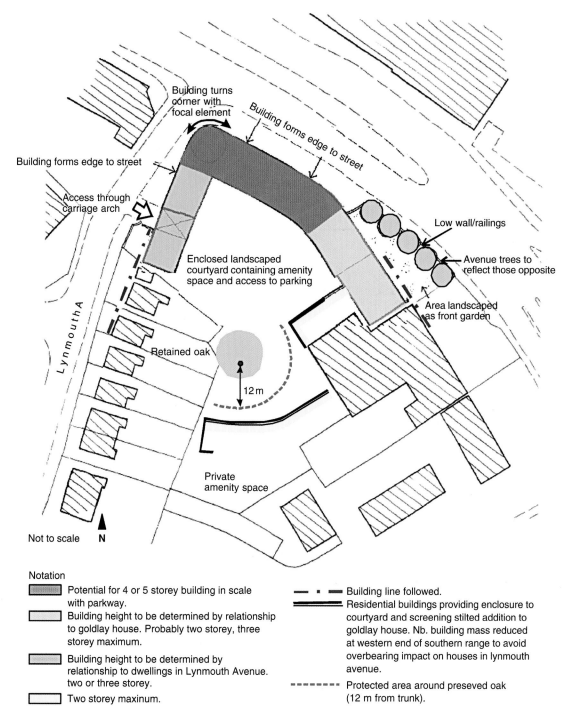

Plate 3.4 Nigel Grogan site brief (CBC, 2003a) – layout principles. Reproduced with the permission of Chelmsford Borough Council and the Ordnance Survey on behalf of HMSO. © Crown copyright 2007. All rights reserved. Licence number 100046642.

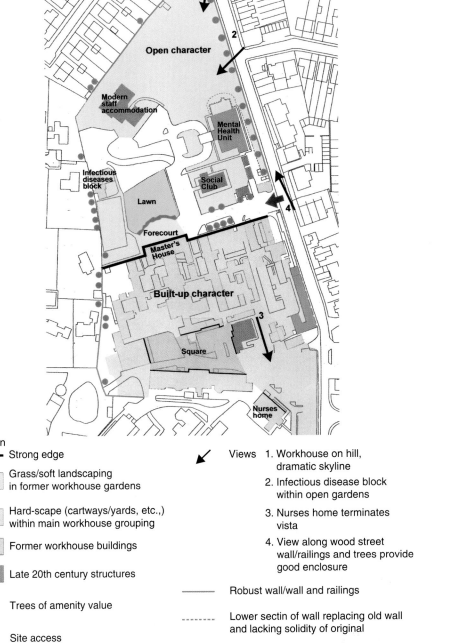

Notation

—— Strong edge

[grass/soft landscaping shading] Grass/soft landscaping in former workhouse gardens

[hard-scape shading] Hard-scape (cartways/yards, etc.,) within main workhouse grouping

[former workhouse buildings shading] Former workhouse buildings

[late 20th century shading] Late 20th century structures

● Trees of amenity value

◀ Site access

↙ Views 1. Workhouse on hill, dramatic skyline

2. Infectious disease block within open gardens

3. Nurses home terminates vista

4. View along wood street wall/railings and trees provide good enclosure

——— Robust wall/wall and railings

--------- Lower sectin of wall replacing old wall and lacking solidity of original

- - - - - Modern 5 m high wall–rear of estates block

Plate 3.5 St John's Hospital character appraisal (CBC, 2003c) – townscape views and spaces. Reproduced with the permission of Chelmsford Borough Council and the Ordnance Survey on behalf of HMSO. © Crown copyright 2007. All rights reserved. Licence number 100046642.

Indicative layout

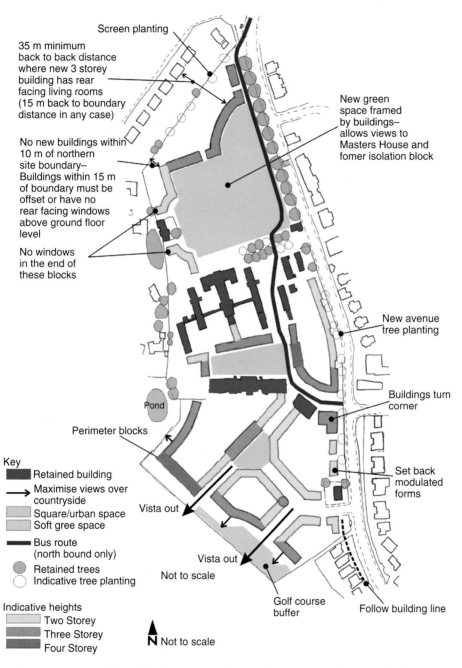

Screen planting

35 m minimum
back to back distance
where new 3 storey
building has rear
facing living rooms
(15 m back to boundary
distance in any case)

No new buildings within
10 m of northern
site boundary–
Buildings within 15 m
of boundary must be
offset or have no
rear facing windows
above ground floor
level

No windows
in the end of
these blocks

New green
space framed
by buildings–
allows views to
Masters House and
fomer isolation block

New avenue
tree planting

Buildings turn
corner

Set back
modulated
forms

Perimeter blocks

Pond

Vista out

Vista out

Golf course
buffer

Follow building line

Key
Retained building
Maximise views over
countryside
Square/urban space
Soft gree space
Bus route
(north bound only)
Retained trees
Indicative tree planting

Not to scale

Indicative heights
Two Storey
Three Storey
Four Storey

N Not to scale

Plate 3.6 St John's Hospital brief (CBC, 2006) – indicative layout. Reproduced with the permission of Chelmsford Borough Council and the Ordnance Survey on behalf of HMSO. © Crown copyright 2007. All rights reserved. Licence number 100046642.

Plate 4.1 The layout produced by Reeves Bailey Architects for the BAe Site. *Source:* Reeves Bailey Architects.

Plate 4.2 The BAe site development approaching completion. Architecture is by Reeves Bailey. Note the provision of small front gardens. *Source:* Chelmsford Borough Council.

Plate 5.1 The layout for the Bishop Mead scheme at chancellor Park prepared by Reeves Bailey Architects for Taylor Woodrow. *Source:* Reeves Bailey Architects.

Plate 5.2   A side street at Bishops Mead, architecture by Reeves Bailey. Note the gates that give access to the rear garages. *Source:* Chelmsford Borough Council.

Plate 5.3   The formal square at the centre of Telford Grange. *Source:* Chelmsford Borough Council.

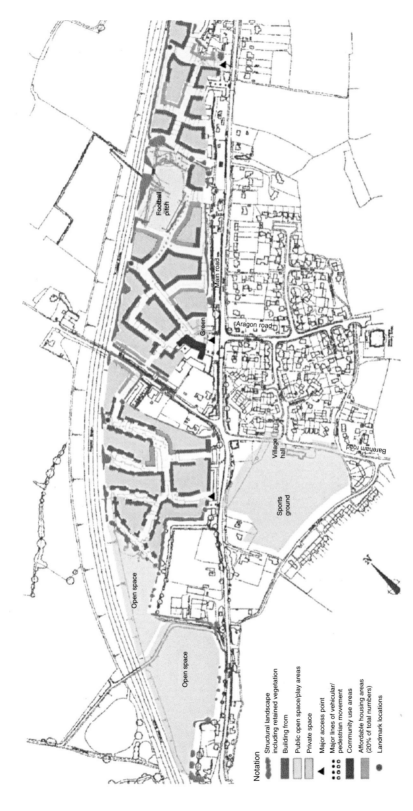

Plate 5.4 Part of the Great Leighs master plan diagram (CBC, 2001b). Note how the structure of blocks and frontages is clearly shown. The light blue colour indicates the location of affordable housing and the purple the location of community facilities. Reproduced with the permission of Chelmsford Borough Council and the Ordnance Survey on behalf of HMSO. © Crown Copyright 2007. All rights reserved. Licence number 100046642.

Notation

- Structural landscape including retained vegetation
- Building from
- Public open space/play areas
- Private space
- Major access point
- Major lines of vehicular/ pedestrian movement
- Community use areas
- Affordable housing areas (20% of total numbers)
- Landmark locations

Football pitch

Main road

Green

Aragon road

Village hall

Barcham road

Sports ground

Open space

Open space

Plate 5.5   An aerial view of phase 1 of the Great Leighs development under construction. *Source:* Peter Rodgers.

Plate 5.6   A view of a side street leading to the main road within phase 1 of the Great Leighs development. *Source:* Tony Hall.

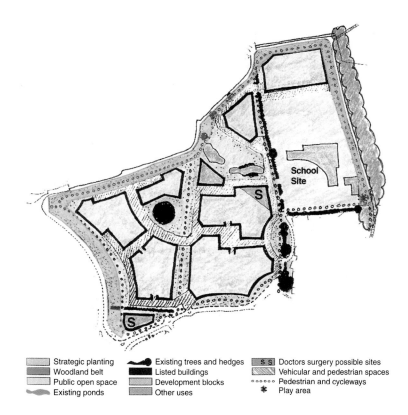

Plate 5.7 The diagram indicating the structure of blocks and open space from the Beaulieu Park North Master Plan (CBC, 2001a). *Source:* Chelmsford Borough Council.

Strategic planting	Existing trees and hedges	S S Doctors surgery possible sites
Woodland belt	Listed buildings	Vehicular and pedestrian spaces
Public open space	Development blocks	Pedestrian and cycleways
Existing ponds	Other uses	✳ Play area

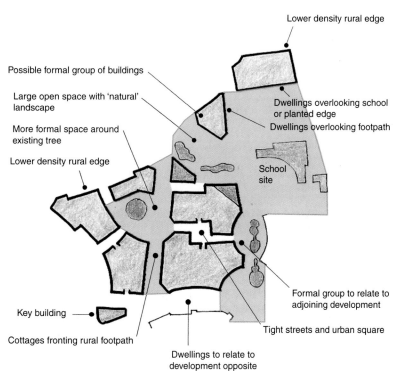

Plate 5.8 The diagram from the Beaulieu Park North Master Plan (CBC, 2001a) showing how character areas should be formed. *Source:* Chelmsford Borough Council.

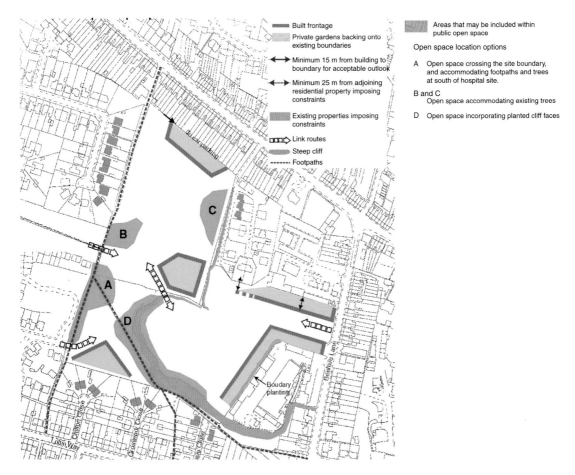

Legend (within figure):

Built frontage

Private gardens backing onto existing boundaries

Minimum 15 m from building to boundary for acceptable outlook

Minimum 25 m from adjoining residential property imposing constraints

Existing properties imposing constraints

Link routes

Steep cliff

Footpaths

Areas that may be included within public open space

Open space location options

A   Open space crossing the site boundary, and accommodating footpaths and trees at south of hospital site.

B and C
Open space accommodating existing trees

D   Open space incorporating planted cliff faces

Plate 5.9   The diagram from the Planning Brief (CBC, 2001b) showing built frontage and open space options for the site of the Clarendon Park scheme. Reproduced with the permission of Chelmsford Borough Council and the Ordnance Survey on behalf of HMSO. © Crown Copyright 2007. All rights reserved. Licence number 100046642.

Plate 5.10 The layout for the Clarendon Park scheme prepared by Robert Hutson Architects for Barratt.

Plate 5.11 The Clarendon Park development showing the relationship to the local open space. *Source:* Tony Hall.

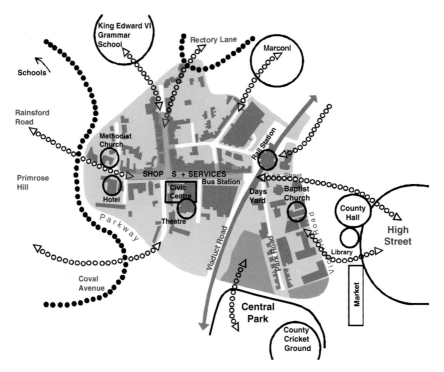

Plate 6.1 The primary land uses and connectivity of the West End. Reproduced with the permission of Chelmsford Borough Council and the Ordnance Survey on behalf of HMSO. © Crown Copyright 2007. All rights reserved. Licence number 100046642.

Plate 6.2 An extract from the West End master plan (CBC, 2000a) showing the proposed reconfiguration of pedestrian spaces. Reproduced with the permission of Chelmsford Borough Council and the Ordnance Survey on behalf of HMSO. © Crown Copyright 2007. All rights reserved. Licence number 100046642.

Plate 7.1 An aerial view of Chelmer Waterside. The river Chelmer can be seen on the left of the picture and the canal basin is to the right. *Source:* Peter Rodgers.

Plate 7.2 Coate's Quay – Phase 2. *Source:* Roy Chandler.

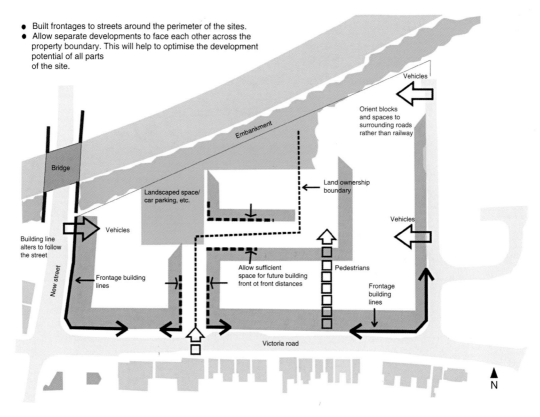

- Built frontages to streets around the perimeter of the sites.
- Allow separate developments to face each other across the property boundary. This will help to optimise the development potential of all parts of the site.

Vehicles

Orient blocks and spaces to surrounding roads rather than railway

Embankment

Bridge

Land ownership boundary

Landscaped space/ car parking, etc.

Vehicles

Building line alters to follow the street

Vehicles

New street

Pedestrians

Frontage building lines

Allow sufficient space for future building front ot front distances

Frontage building lines

Victoria road

N

Plate 7.3 The diagram from planning brief (CBC, 2002e) for the site of Capital Square development showing the desired arrangement of blocks, frontages and open space. *Source:* Chelmsford Borough Council.

Willow Court

Most of the infill schemes that were in Chelmsford were not, though, of the scale and density as seen at Writtle Road. An important example of a smaller-scale scheme from this period was the redevelopment of part of the Foreman's works, a disused factory site in the west of the urban area. The first proposal for the site, late in 1998, did not provide adequate rear gardens or sufficient continuous frontage, nor did it take full advantage of the site's southerly views over parkland. The problem was not that it was poor compared with what had been built up to 1998 – it certainly was not – but that it did not meet the high standards now expected. It was refused planning permission and a subsequent appeal was dismissed in late 1999. The site was then sold on to Bellway, who, in discussion with the Borough's urban design officers, provided a new layout incorporating a marginally higher density with more continuity of frontage. It now addressed the parkland in a more satisfactory manner although further negotiations were necessary to ensure that the dwellings took maximum advantage of the view. The result, called Willow Court by the developers, was an urban scheme that not only met the council's policies but also fitted its context and created an attractive sense of place. It was completed in 2000. Figure 5.16 shows the layout and Figure 5.17 shows the southerly aspect facing the park.

Telford Grange

Another interesting example was the redevelopment, also by Bellway, of a former college site which they later called Telford Grange. As the site had become available at comparatively short notice, its layout was guided by an officer-produced concept statement (CBC, 1999a). The design principles were summarised within this document by a diagram, which is reproduced as Figure 5.18. The concept statement also set out the design principles in words and used diagrams to convey possible alternative block and open-space arrangements. Much negotiation then proved necessary, particularly to ensure that the houses addressed the adjacent allotments and made the use of proper corner types. Achieving this end required not only clever use of the developer's existing house designs but a new design based on one taken from the array of house types suggested in the appendix to the Essex guide (EPOA, 1997). Eventually, the layout illustrated in Figure 5.19 was agreed to, and it received planning permission in 2001. It contained 49 dwellings, featured continuous frontage, as shown in Figure 5.20, and incorporated the rectangular, formal open space shown in Figure 5.21.

What was interesting about this particular development was how it illustrated the transition from the use of developers' standard house-types to designs that, if not designed specifically for the particular site, were designed to facilitate the required urban form. Although, on close inspection, it could be seen that that some of the frontages were composed of standard house-types welded together, and that the standard of architectural detailing could have been higher in places, the development, nevertheless, achieved a compact form that provided a pleasant place to live. Although perhaps not of the same standard as Bishops Mead, Telford Grange and, even more so, Willow Court represented a considerable advance on other developments that had gone before.

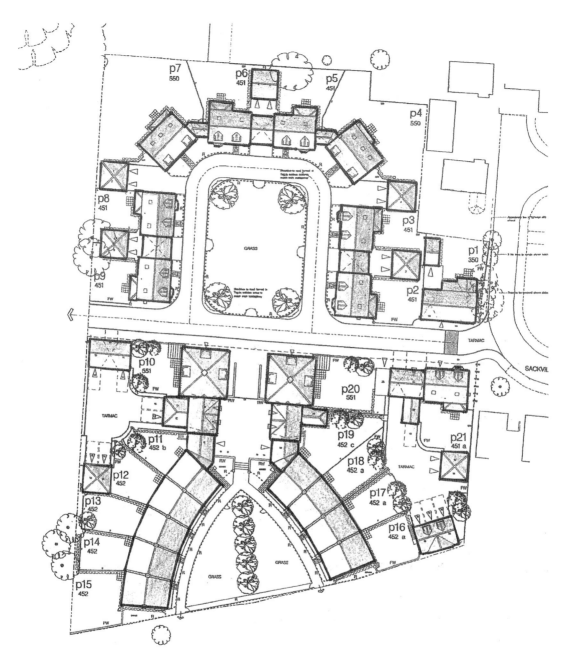

Figure 5.16 The layout for Willow Court by Bellway Homes. Reproduced with the permission of Bellway Homes.

Figure 5.17 The town houses fronting the park at Willow Court. *Source:* Chelmsford Borough Council.

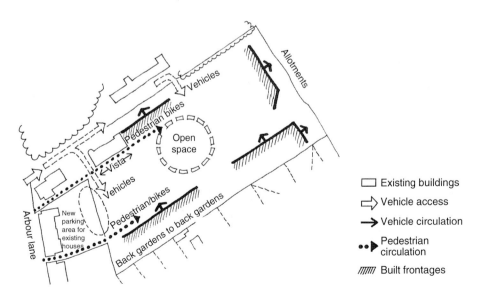

Figure 5.18 Diagram showing the development principles from the Concept Statement (CBC, 1999a) for the site of Telford Grange. *Source:* Chelmsford Borough Council.

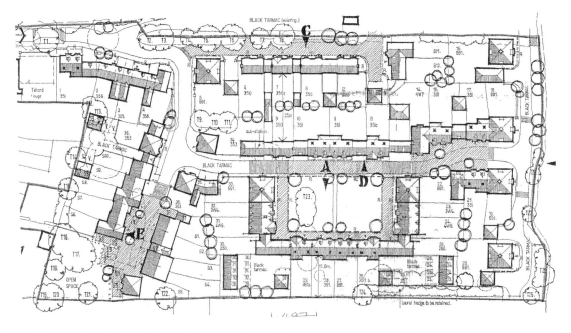

Figure 5.19   The layout for Telford Grange by Bellway Homes. *Source:* Bellway Homes.

Figure 5.20   A side street in Telford Grange. Note the provision of small front gardens. *Source:* Chelmsford Borough Council.

Figure 5.21   The formal square at the centre of Telford Grange. See also Plate 5.3. *Source:* Chelmsford Borough Council.

The mature process: 2000–2003

As Chelmsford entered the new millennium, the position had been reached where every residential development was expected to achieve, and did achieve, the required standards. The council's urban design team was approaching full strength and was applying its accumulated experience in negotiation to each proposal that came forward. Each site where development was imminent now had a design brief prepared well in advance, which outlined the physical structure for development. During the period from 2001 to 2003, a new Borough plan (CBC, 2001a) was on deposit. It contained the substantial and detailed design policies set out in Chapter 2 on page 38 of. In legal terms, it constituted a material consideration when determining applications for planning permission, and as the design policies had attracted few objections, they carried a significant degree of weight. The following examples illustrate how the process worked, as does the example described at the end of Chapter 4, page 77. These represent, however, only a selection from a large number of similar schemes.

Great Leighs

A significant area of land was allocated for housing in the 1991–2001 Borough plan (CBC, 1997a) in association with the proposed construction of a bypass west of Great Leighs, a village 7 mi (11 km) north of the town centre. The proposal was originally for a village extension of 150 dwellings. A very general planning brief was published in 1996 (CBC, 1996c), similar in content to the briefs for the other sites, which were published at that time. Planning permission was conditional upon the construction of the bypass, which, in the event, did not take place until 2002. The whole development was, therefore, subject to a far greater degree of design control, and took place at a much higher density than would have been the case if building had started in the mid-1990s.

The land was acquired by David Wilson Homes. The outline planning permission from 1997 required the preparation of a master plan, but serious work on it did not start until the go-ahead had been given for the bypass. David Wilson Homes' first efforts at a master plan rang alarm bells with the Council's officers. It was based on a series of culs-de-sac off a spine road, with awkward links and no sense of built structure. The urban design team then took a leading role in developing a joint master plan with David Wilson Homes and their consultants. The discussions started by coming to an understanding of the linkages and routes through what was a difficult and narrow site. They continued by experimenting with the structure and location of spaces. As the structure evolved, the urban design team used informal sketches and critiques to work out a layout and looked at the practicality of different approaches. An example of the results of one such session is shown in Figure 5.22. Figure 5.23 shows how the block structure of Phase 2 of the scheme evolved by stages. This led to the layout for Phase 2 shown in Figure 5.24, a structure based on perimeter blocks and clear routes, and with a series of different types of spaces.

The original, and very general, planning brief from 1996 (CBC, 1996c) was eventually replaced by a master plan drawn up, not just by the developer, David Wilson Homes, but by the urban designers of the Borough Council working with them. In contrast to the content of the developer produced 'master plans' of the mid-1990s, it set out a structure of urban spaces and blocks, rather than roads. Negotiations with the developer were successful to such a degree

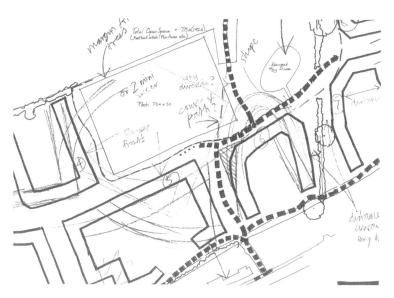

Figure 5.22 An example of a working sketch produced during negotiations on the Great Leighs layout. *Source:* Chelmsford Borough Council.

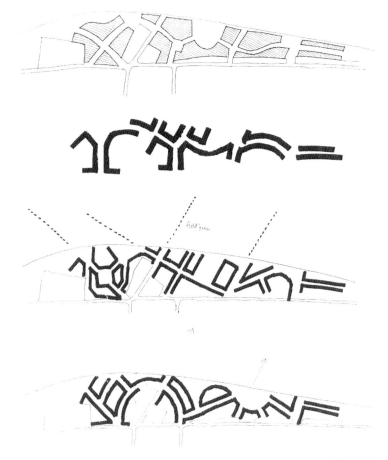

Figure 5.23 Examples of working sketches showing the evolution of block forms through the negotiations on Great Leighs. *Source:* Chelmsford Borough Council.

that, by the time of its final publication of the master plan (CBC, 2001b), they could add their own logo to the cover as a sign of their assent. The quality of the results brought about by these negotiations between the design team and the developer can be seen from the diagram in the published master plan shown in Figure 5.25.

David Wilson Homes' original detailed layout for Phase 2 had been fragmented, illegible, had a poor sense of space and was dominated by culs-de-sac. Figure 5.26 shows the layout that was eventually granted planning permission. It demonstrated legibility, perimeter blocks with secluded private areas, character areas and clear routes. Higher densities of 34 dph in Phases 2 and 3 had resulted in total of 329 dwellings being provided and a much tighter urban form than would have been the case if the development had occurred earlier. Figure 5.27 shows an aerial view the first phase of the development under construction. Figures 5.28. 5.29 and 5.30 show street scenes within it, and Figure 5.31 shows its frontage to the main road.

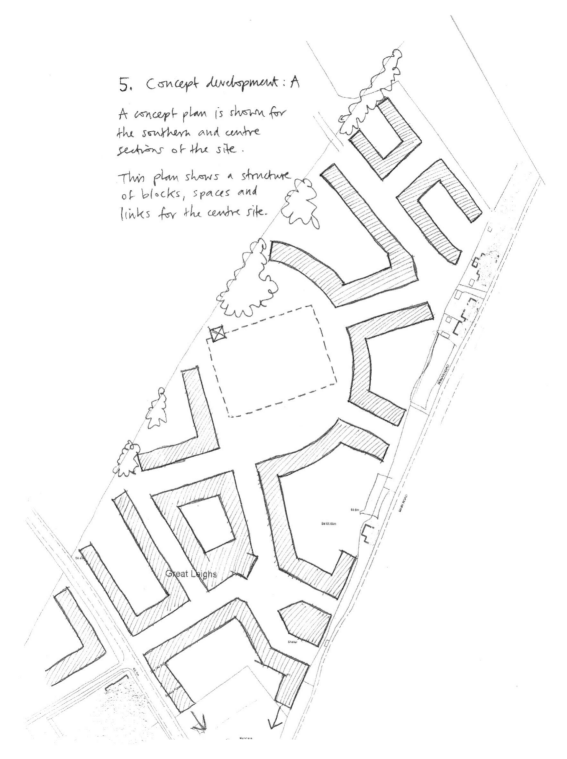

5. Concept development: A

A concept plan is shown for the southern and centre sections of the site.

This plan shows a structure of blocks, spaces and links for the centre site.

Great Leighs

Figure 5.24 An example of a concept plan produced during negotiations on block forms for Great Leighs. *Source:* Chelmsford Borough Council.

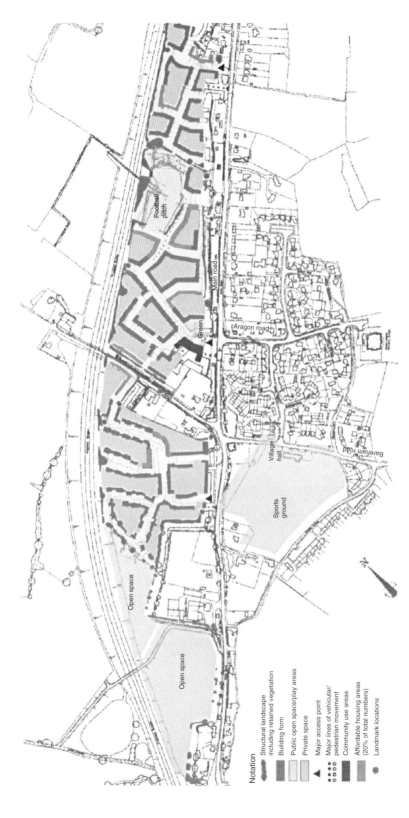

Figure 5.25 Part of the Great Leighs master plan diagram (CBC, 2001b). Note how the structure of blocks and frontages is clearly shown. See also Plate 5.4. Reproduced with the permission of Chelmsford Borough Council and the Ordnance Survey on behalf of HMSO. © Crown Copyright 2007. All rights reserved. Licence number 100046642.

Notation

- Structural landscape including retained vegetation
- Building form
- Public open space/play areas
- Private space
- Major access point
- Major lines of vehicular/ pedestrian movement
- Community use areas
- Affordable housing areas (20% of total numbers)
- Landmark locations

Football pitch

Main road

Green

Aragon road

Village hall

Bareham road

Sports ground

Open space

Open space

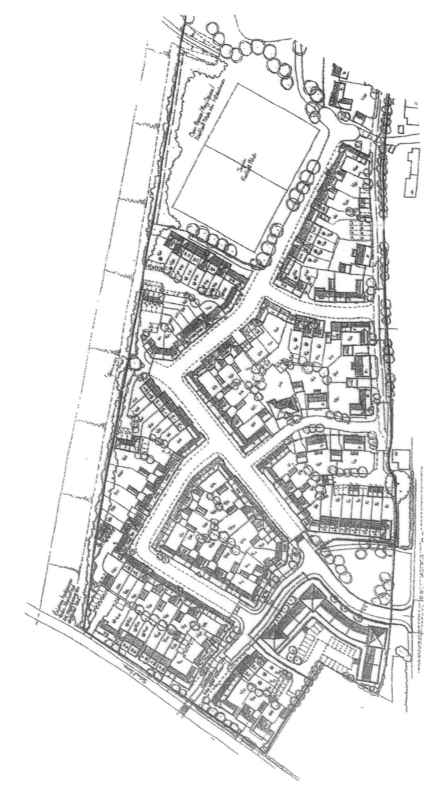

Figure 5.26 The detailed layout for phase 2 of the Great Leighs development by David Wilson Homes. Note the close correspondence to the Master Plan extract in Figure 5.25. Reproduced with the permission of David Wilson Homes.

Figure 5.27 An aerial view of phase 1 of the Great Leighs development under construction. See also Plate 5.5. *Source:* Peter Rodgers.

Figure 5.28 The street at the centre of phase 1 of the Great Leighs development. *Source:* Tony Hall.

Figure 5.29 A view of a side street leading to the main road within phase 1 of the Great Leighs development. See also Plate 5.6. *Source:* Tony Hall.

Figure 5.30 A view of a side street shown in Figure 5.29 linking to the main road. *Source:* Tony Hall.

Figure 5.31 The frontage of phase 1 of the Great Leighs development to main road. *Source:* Tony Hall.

Beaulieu Park North

The central and southern sections of Beaulieu Park were developed first and were subject to the gradual increase in residential density and standards of design described on page 99. Given the complexity created by the sale of different sections of the site to different developers, and the general skeletal nature of both the original brief (CBC, 1996b) and Countryside Properties' own original master Plan, by 2000 it was clear that a new master plan for the northern part of the site was required. This new document (CBC, 2001c) was part of Chelmsford's new generation of planning guidance. The text provided a systematic appraisal of the site and included the new, and strongly prescriptive, master plan diagram shown in Figure 5.32. Note the specification of blocks, frontages, pedestrian routes and local open space. A further diagram, shown in Figure 5.33 identified the character areas that were to be provided within the urban form.

The result was that the urban form of Beaulieu Park North was different not only from the first stage, described on page 93, but also from the intermediate stage, described on page 99. Gone was the use of larger dwellings and neoclassical styles. The houses were smaller, almost entirely in neovernacular style and continuity of frontage was maintained throughout. There was effective integration of affordable housing. Street scenes within the completed development are shown in Figures 5.34 and 5.35. Figure 5.34 shows part of the integrated affordable housing.

Strategic planting | Existing trees and hedges | **S** Doctors surgery possible sites
Woodland belt | Listed buildings | Vehicular and pedestrian spaces
Public open space | Development blocks | Pedestrian and cycleways
Existing ponds | Other uses | ✽ Play area

Figure 5.32 The diagram indicating the structure of blocks and open space from the Beaulieu Park North Master Plan (CBC, 2001a). See also Plate 5.7. *Source:* Chelmsford Borough Council.

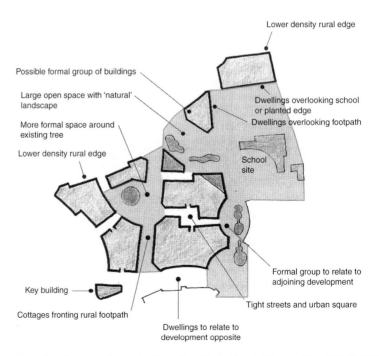

Lower density rural edge

Possible formal group of buildings

Large open space with 'natural' landscape

Dwellings overlooking school or planted edge

More formal space around existing tree

Dwellings overlooking footpath

Lower density rural edge

School site

Key building

Formal group to relate to adjoining development

Cottages fronting rural footpath

Tight streets and urban square

Dwellings to relate to development opposite

Figure 5.33 The diagram from the Beaulieu Park North Master Plan (CBC, 2001a) showing how character areas should be formed. See also Plate 5.8. *Source:* Chelmsford Borough Council.

Figure 5.34 A view of part of the social housing within Beaulieu Park North. Note the arrangements for paving and planting. *Source:* Chelmsford Borough Council.

Figure 5.35 Housing within Beaulieu Park North fronting a local open space.

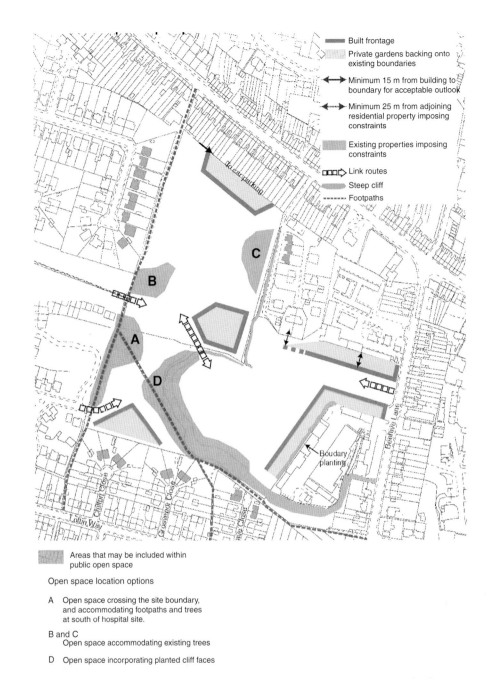

Built frontage

Private gardens backing onto existing boundaries

Minimum 15 m from building to boundary for acceptable outlook

Minimum 25 m from adjoining residential property imposing constraints

Existing properties imposing constraints

Link routes

Steep cliff

Footpaths

Areas that may be included within public open space

Open space location options

A   Open space crossing the site boundary, and accommodating footpaths and trees at south of hospital site.

B and C
    Open space accommodating existing trees

D   Open space incorporating planted cliff faces

Figure 5.36   The diagram from the Planning Brief (CBC, 2001b) showing built frontage and open space options for the site of the Clarendon Park scheme. See also Plate 5.9. Reproduced with the permission of Chelmsford Borough Council and the Ordnance Survey on behalf of HMSO. © Crown Copyright 2007. All rights reserved. Licence number 100046642.

Figure 5.37 The layout for the Clarendon Park scheme prepared by Robert Hutson Architects for Barratt. See also Plate 5.10.

Clarendon Park

At the eastern end of the original Princes Road and Moulsham Lodge housing land allocation in the 1997 Borough plan (CBC, 1997a) was a disused hospital site. This site took a long time to come forward for development and construction did not eventually start until 2002. The delay was fortuitous as the site was not included in the low standard and controversial development of 1997–1998 but was now subject to the post-2000 policy regime. It was, somewhat ironically, bought by Barratt who had started the development of this land allocation north of Princes Road in 1996, as related at the beginning of this chapter on page 87. The contrast between that development, shown in Figure 5.1, and what was to be built here was to prove dramatic and showed just how far the planning process had come. Although the site was, in principle, still subject to the original 1996 Princes Road and Moulsham Lodge brief (CBC, 1996a), a new brief was produced and approved in 2002 (CBC, 2002a) for the eastern sector. This was of the new generation of briefs, those that gave attention to the location of block forms. The layout principles are shown by Figure 5.36, but it is important to remember that this is only one diagram from a substantial document. The process of design control was now working, as it should, with full co-operation from the developer. Their agents produced a full design statement, which was still a rare occurrence at that time. The final layout is shown in Figure 5.37. Views of the development as constructed, called Clarendon Park by the developers, are shown in Figures 5.38 and 5.39. The resultant built

Figure 5.38 The Clarendon Park development showing the relationship to the local open space. See also Plate 5.11. *Source:* Tony Hall.

Figure 5.39 A side street within the Clarendon Park development. *Source:* Tony Hall.

form was a success and represented another step forward. Although the same criticisms of architectural details as were made of Telford Grange could be applied here, what was laudable was the treatment of the public spaces. A connected sequence of more informal spaces, laid to grass and defined by different building types, created important legibility and character. Given that this was a difficult sloping site with very limited vehicular access, this was a significant achievement.

Chapter 6

Pursuing an urban renaissance

Challenges and opportunities

A contemporary visitor to Chelmsford would be struck by the economic and social vitality of the town centre – prosperous shops and a lively public realm. Whatever may, or may not, have been the case in the past, recent construction shows a high standard of design. New buildings exhibit a range of styles relating to their context. There are now a substantial number of people living in the central area, on what was brownfield land, in buildings designed by architects to fit the site. Many of them are living in mixed-use schemes over shops facing the street. However, far from being inevitable, in the early and mid-1990s all this would have seemed a most unlikely prospect.

In the early to mid-1970s, the centre of the town had been subjected to substantial and insensitive redevelopment. A key element of the planning of the time was the construction of a dual carriageway inner relief road to the south and west of the town centre known as Parkway. Such roads were, of course, to be found in many British towns of this period and they brought with them some the same disadvantages. Despite improvements to traffic flow, the road paid no heed to the existing street pattern and the links between the centre and the rest of the town to the south and west were severed. Buses, cyclists and pedestrians had to take circuitous routes to get to and from the shopping centre. The council allowed, and indeed encouraged, the building of a new shopping complex, now known as High Chelmer, with the loss of some significant historic buildings and townscape. The architecture of this new shopping centre was routine and bland. It focused inwards on new pedestrian shopping routes and turned its back on the existing shopping centre. An extremely large and visually intrusive multi-storey car park was constructed between the new shopping centre and Parkway. This period also saw the building of a number of unloved and visually intrusive office blocks, one of which dominates the views of the town centre to this day.*

*It can be seen in the background of Figure 6.21.

In 1990, another large new shopping complex, the Meadows, had been completed, which, although adequate for its purpose, did not exhibit the highest standards of design. Although it had active frontage to the High Street, it did not have active frontage to the rear, where it adjoined the town's rivers. It had been located on the opposite side of the centre to the High Chelmer shops and had brought with it a fear that the centre of gravity of retailing was moving east, to the detriment of activity on the western side of the town centre.

Local planning policies drawn up during the late 1980s had envisaged a further large shopping complex to the east of the High Street, in conjunction with further large multi-storey car parks and access roads. However, none of these proposals had come about because of a lack of finance. The growth of edge-of-town retail facilities, and the building in the early 1990s of the large Lakeside out-of-town shopping and leisure complex in the south of Essex, had created a feeling of pessimism about the long-term prosperity of existing centres in Essex and the continuity of major investment was not forthcoming. Some developers sought permission for low-intensity retail uses. Others obtained permission for new office blocks. In general, they did not appear to be yet aware that the market for major new office blocks had begun to decline. In the event, these blocks were either delayed for substantial periods or not built at all.

There were, however, opportunities in the town centre waiting to be grasped. There was a substantial concentration of employment in retailing, public administration, financial services and higher education. This provided trade for the shops and suggested the possibility of short journeys to work on foot for those who could live there once suitable dwellings had been provided. The expanded shopping provision appeared resilient to out-of-town competition. High Street had been pedestrianised during 1998–1990 and this scheme was to be extended. The university had started to move to a new site on the edge of the town centre. This not only would create more employment and student activity but would also provide opportunities for innovative design. It would also release, in the longer term, a large and important site for redevelopment adjacent to the railway station. The bus station was also awaiting redevelopment. There were extensive areas of surface car parks on former industrial land now owned by the Borough Council. Much of this land was intersected by a system of waterways made up of a confluence of two rivers and a canal that provided a potential amenity waiting to be accessed. Most significant of all was the high, and increasing, level of demand for new housing.

The precursors of change

River valley enhancement

The improvement of the river valleys, or 'green wedges' as they became known in local planning documents, is one Chelmsford success story that was achieved not so much through the changes of the late 1990s but more by gradual change over a longer period. Chelmsford had the advantage of shallow river valleys that had remained largely free of development outside of the town centre. One valley bisected the town completely, east to west, and one ran northwards from the centre. From the centre eastwards, the river was joined by the Chelmer and Blackwater Canal. They had the potential to form 'greenways' connecting the suburbs to, and through, the town centre. In this respect, they were an important component of the revitalisation of the centre. Although opportunities had not always been grasped in Chelmsford, this one had been.

The provision of cycle ways and footpaths started in the 1980s, as did the purchase of land by the Borough Council for playing fields and parks. Much of the land was undefended flood plain for which development was not easy and would not, nowadays, be considered desirable. Funding from development to the north-east of the town in the late 1970s provided a footpath cycle way linking it to the town centre via the eastern valley. The provision of this, and other footpath cycle ways, was not just a matter of providing routes but involved the acquisition and landscaping of green space on either side. From the early 1980s onwards, commuted payments for strategic open space were available for the laying out of new playing fields and these were consolidated in the northern valley. The gradual redevelopment of the town centre, waterside areas and university campus opened up new links between the valleys through the centre of town. The eastern valley, together with its canal, was made a conservation area in 1991.

When combined with fields still in agricultural use, parks, playing fields and the rivers themselves, all these steps created a wider landscape with a high standard of amenity over a wide area. The resulting quality of the environment positively encouraged walking and cycling as pleasurable activities. As a regular user in the past of the footpaths for the journey to work, the author can attest personally to the pleasant ambience and high degree of usage.

Retention of food stores

One important issue for contemporary town centres is the retention of provision for the sale of food and other groceries. The provision of new and expanded supermarkets in suburban and edge-of-town locations has often threatened the survival of smaller stores in older centres. Where there is no provision for the sale of groceries in a town centre this reduces the opportunity for the combination of different types of shopping trip and can thereby reduce the general level of activity and vitality of a centre. It also reduces the opportunities for those who cannot, or do not wish to, use a car and is a disincentive for people to return to live in the centre.

In the 1970s, Chelmsford's town centre had three small supermarkets, run by Sainsbury, Tesco and the Co-op. The Sainsbury store closed following the building of an edge-of-town store in the early 1990s. The rebuilding of the small Co-op store is described, under the heading of West End regeneration, on page 143.

A positive step in the early 1980s was the building of a new Tesco town-centre supermarket. This was, for its time, a full-size supermarket with full car parking provision, located on what was then the edge of the town centre. What was unusual for the period, and remarkably beneficial as events were to turn out, was that the building was aligned with the street frontage, some of it active frontage, and with parking above and behind, as opposed to the common practice of having car parking in front. The car parking on the roof gave height to what would otherwise have been a single-storey structure and improved its contribution to the street scene. The amount of car parking made it commercially successful and encouraged a symbiotic relationship with the rest of the town centre. By buying a certain amount of groceries customers could park for free and then walk into the town centre for other shopping and refreshments. This ensured both the continued presence of significant food retailing in the town centre in the long term and enhanced the town centre's general commercial attractiveness. The supermarket has been retained despite the provision of a very large suburban facility by the same retailer in the early 1990s.

Conservation of historical features

Another common issue in retaining, and enhancing, the quality of a town centre is the retention of historical features. Although they may be seen in some quarters as an impediment to the expansion of retail facilities, they can add to the overall distinction and sense of place and play a positive role in attracting custom.

In Chelmsford, one valuable change for the better occurred at the very end of the 1980s. The 19th-century Grays Brewery building, long disused as such, was

Figure 6.1 The Grays Brewery redevelopment. The building to the left formed part of the original 19th-century brewery. The building at the back of the picture forms part of the Meadows shopping complex. *Source:* Roy Chandler.

saved from demolition though the initiative of an Essex County Council officer and an unexpected grant of listed-building protection by the government. It was converted into a small shopping complex with a new pedestrian space in front, connected to the adjacent department store by escalator. The result, shown in Figure 6.1, was not just the retention of a small memento of Chelmsford's heritage but a positive contribution to character, legibility and sense of place of this part of its centre.

Figure 6.2 An aerial view of the High Street pedestrianisation scheme. *Source:* Barry Knight.

Figure 6.3 Two street views of the High Street pedestrianisation scheme. *Source:* Anglia Ruskin University.

High Street pedestrianisation and a new shopping complex

The most substantial alterations to the shopping centre since the 1970s took place around 1989–1990. These were the pedestrianisation of the High Street, shown in Figures 6.2 and 6.3, and the construction of the Meadows shopping complex. The two schemes occurred together and have made a net positive contribution to the subsequent commercial success of the town centre. Certainly the pedestrianisation was an essential requirement. Little could have been achieved subsequently without it. It was facilitated by the construction of a new bridge over the river, which removed the through traffic. This bridge also provided servicing access to the Meadows centre and was paid for out of the proceeds of the development. The Meadows complex added a substantial amount of fully enclosed retail floor space to the town centre, with access points to both the existing High Street, shown in Figure 6.4, to new walkways along the rivers and a substantial amount of short-stay car parking. This being said, the design of both, while superior to what had been built in the 1970s, was not of a standard that would have been permitted a decade later. Officer intervention ensured a rear high-level goods access for the Meadows, enabling it to have a limited amount of active frontage to the rivers and full frontage to the High Street. Nevertheless, the sides of the development along the new river walkways were, for much of their length, blank walls. The disappointing aspect of the pedestrianisation scheme was the poor overall design of the paving, planting and street furniture.

Figure 6.4   The entrance to the Meadows shopping centre from the High Street.
Source: Chelmsford Borough Council.

An area of disused land on the other side of the River Chelmer was developed at the same time to form a second stage of the Meadows scheme. Unfortunately, although the new retail units had frontage both to the pedestrianised street and a new river walkway, they were, to put it mildly, architecturally undistinguished. They were more typical of a low-intensity, edge-of-town location and did not anticipate the way that land values were to increase. The rear of the development lacked height. The side next to the new road bridge could, on aesthetic grounds alone, have taken significantly taller buildings. This was an example of how mistakes, or at least lack of vision, can create developments that are not only poor in themselves but can frustrate the process of both commercial growth and better design in the longer term.

The changes begin

By the mid-to-late 1990s, it was becoming clear that the earlier pessimism about commercial prospects was no longer justified. Rather than needing to be protected from decline, the centre was prospering. Demand for more sophisticated retailing was increasing, but the biggest change was the growth in restaurants, bars and nightclubs. This was driven by the increasing numbers of people moving into the town and the fact that some were now beginning to live near to, or even inside, the central area. The combination of shops with places for entertainment and refreshment not only broadened the general attractiveness of the town centre but also caused people to stay within it for longer periods. The increasing use of information technology for the management of storage and servicing lessened the need for storage space and meant that the physical constraints of traditional centres were not as much of a problem when offering a range products and services. From the perspective of the evolution of both design and retail policy, the fact that the massive extension of retail and parking provision on land to the east of the High Street, and elsewhere, envisioned in the early 1990s, had not occurred was to prove fortuitous by permitting a different approach to be followed.

Improving the paving

Although the pedestrianisation of the High Street had been welcome and formed an essential foundation for the continuing prosperity of the centre, the brick paving, the planters and the street furniture could have been much better handled. An opportunity for an improvement occurred in 1996 when the repaving of a short section of street in the centre, Baddow Road, was carried out. It was fronted by two-storey structures going back over several centuries and occupied by restaurants and small shops. The traffic circulation arrangements put in for the parking facilities for the Meadows centre precluded, unfortunately, full pedestrianisation. However, an enhancement scheme enlarged the pedestrian space and greatly improved the quality of the paving, with the support of English Heritage. York stone was used where appropriate. Public art was also introduced. The finished result is illustrated in Figure 6.5.

Style and architectural quality

As with the residential development discussed in Chapter 5, planning intervention in matters of style was seen as not as a constraint but, on the contrary, as a stimulus to higher architectural standards. To put it more plainly, when the planners took a strong line, funding for quality and thence scope for the architect were more likely to be forthcoming. This argument applied equally to the residential development in the central area described in Chapter 7. The question of appropriateness of style was very much one of context, reflecting both the existing physical form and the nature of the commercial, retail and entertainment activities. It was not, in any sense, random or arbitrary.

Although the greater part of the urban area as a whole was a product of the 20th century, the town centre revealed aspects of many periods from the town's 2000-year history. In some parts there were buildings of a domestic scale that had grown by accretion since mediaeval times. In others, there were examples of 19th-century manufacture, such as the Grays Brewery, shown in Figure 6.1. In contrast, the 20th-century history of the town provided modern, or even

Figure 6.5 The section of Baddow Road within the town centre repaved with the use of York stone to increase the space for pedestrians while retaining vehicle access. *Source:* Chelmsford Borough Council.

high-tech, themes based on Marconi, the birth of the radio and subsequent growth of the electronics industry.

As the prosperity of the town centre increased, some premises were demolished and rebuilt. Although there was no overriding stylistic character for the centre as a whole, negotiations by design officers used the reconstruction and refurbishment to create frontages that, in some cases conserved 19th-century character, or reflected older traditions, while not interfering with contemporary retail commercial requirements. In other cases, the construction of buildings of architectural quality in modern styles was welcomed.

The first significant physical consequence of this policy was the building, in 2002, of the small row of shops shown in Figure 6.6. Following positive negotiations between the developers and the council's urban design officers, it was designed in a neovernacular style with small units and active frontage. The scale and style were determined by its position at the end of Baddow Road, the street of historic buildings hosting small shops shown in Figure 6.4. The interesting

Figure 6.6 New shops at Can Bridge Way in a neovernacular style. The street shown in Figure 6.6 is to the left of the view; the vehicle entrance to the parking for the Meadows shopping complex is to the right. *Source:* Chelmsford Borough Council.

point is that the result could easily have been different, as the site was also on the corner of an approach road to the car parks to the rear of the Meadows centre, known as Can Bridge Way.

Infill with new shops in a distinctly modern style can be seen in Figure 6.7. In contrast to the situation at Can Bridge Way, here the location was the High Street with large stores exhibiting fronts from a variety of more recent periods.

Refreshment and entertainment

The first and second stages of Meadows development opened up the side of the river known as French's Walk. Before and after views looking down-river are shown in Figure 6.8(a) and (b). It was, unfortunately, fronted by poorly conceived buildings that did not necessarily contribute to a new urban lifestyle. However, the new pedestrian spaces by the river and new linkages that were opened up provided, fortuitously, a space in which daytime and night-time, pedestrian and pavement life could flourish, if infill and incremental improvements were properly steered. Figures 6.9 and 6.10 show views of what French's Walk became.

The increasing rate of growth in demand for public houses catering to young people, both in their roles as nightspots in their own right and as precursors to visits to nightclubs, posed more of a dilemma. It was one of the foremost sources of trade for town-centre expansion and could provide refreshment facilities complementary to shopping in the daytime. However, the night-time trade also

Figure 6.7 Replacement of High Street shops in a contemporary style. *Source:* Anglia Ruskin University.

had the potential to cause disturbance. Fortunately, the matter resolved itself spatially by both good fortune and design. The sites that became available were not near any dwellings and clustering occurred in one area centred around French's Walk. Although negotiation played a part, this was to the commercial advantage of the operators as young people tended to walk from bar to bar and then on to the nightclubs. Figure 6.10 looks up-river towards the area that became the focus for bars and restaurants. The first stage of the Meadows complex is to the left and the second stage to the right.

In this part of the town-centre there was an awkwardly shaped piece of land by the river shown in Figure 6.11(a). The site had a little access and had remained unused for 30 years. As with other sites in Chelmsford, the delay proved fortuitous

Figure 6.8 (a) The view down river before the construction of the Meadows shopping complex. *Source:* Chelmsford Borough Council. (b) The view shown in (a) after redevelopment. Phase 1 of the Meadows development is to the right and phase 2 is to the left. *Source:* Rodger Tamblyn.

Figure 6.9 Backnang Square and the pavement cafés in French's Walk. *Source:* Chelmsford Borough Council.

in terms of design policies. The site was eventually developed by Countryside Properties in a strikingly modern manner. The glass-walled building is illustrated in Figure 6.11 (b) and 6.12 and can be seen at the centre of Figure 6.10. It contained bars and restaurants and offered near total transparency and river frontage. The building's curved glass front integrated well with the river. A pocket urban

Figure 6.10 French's Walk looking upstream towards the area of concentration of bars and restaurants. *Source:* Rodger Tamblyn.

Figure 6.11 (a) The side of the difficult site of the new bar complex before redevelopment. (b) The side of the new bar complex as constructed. *Source:* Chelmsford Borough Council.

space was created on the road frontage and shared surfaces for pedestrians and cyclists on the river frontage, as can be seen from Figure 6.12. The development opened up the river frontage, provided a new landmark and was commercially successful.

Re-creation of active frontage

On the opposite bank of the river was a 1960s office building with ground floor shops that had become difficult to let. Its southern end can be seen in Figure 6.11(a). In previous decades, planning policy would have sought to protect and preserve these uses. However, planning permission was granted

Figure 6.12 The front view of the new bar complex. *Source:* Chelmsford Borough Council.

for a restaurant at the building's northern end and for a bar at the southern end opposite the Countryside Properties development. The urban design officers now promoted the idea of extending this bar at the back of the building on two levels, thus providing active frontage to the river and footpath-cycle way as shown in Figures 6.11(b) and 6.13.

From 2000 onwards, the design officers also pressed retailers on the other side of the Meadows complex to establish cafés and kiosks that opened up the previously blank facades to riverside pedestrian spaces. Figures 6.14 and 6.15 show before and after views of the provision of a small shop. Figure 6.16 and 6.17 show before and after views of the opening out of an existing café to provide active frontage to the river. The wider part of French's Walk, now named Backnang Square, became the home of pavement cafés on a much grander scale as shown in Figures 6.9 and 6.10.

A pavement society

In addition to the experience at French's Walk, the growth of pavement cafés in the High Street, and surrounding streets, also took off. The process began around 2000 and they increased in number year after year. These facilities proved complementary to the retail function and have encouraged shoppers to prolong their visits and engage in a package of shopping, eating and entertainment activities in pleasant surroundings. Figure 6.18 shows the pavement cafés in the vicinity of the historic Shire Hall at the northern end of the pedestrianised High Street. Figure 6.19 shows similar cafés at the southern end.

Figure 6.13 The rear extension for the bar and restaurant located on the ground floor of an older office building. (The southern end of the same building can also be seen in Figures 6.10 and 6.11).

Figure 6.14 The Meadows frontage to French's Walk in its original state. *Source:* Chelmsford Borough Council.

Figure 6.15 The Meadows frontage to French's Walk following the addition of a small shop. *Source:* Chelmsford Borough Council.

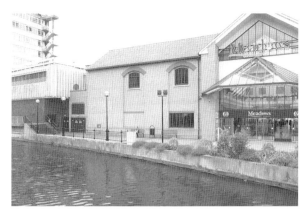

Figure 6.16 The Meadows frontage to the river in its original state. *Source:* Chelmsford Borough Council.

Figure 6.17 The Meadows frontage to the river with a cafe inside the shopping complex opened out on to the footway. *Source:* Chelmsford Borough Council.

Figure 6.18 Pavement cafés at the Shire Hall end of the High Street. *Source:* Chelmsford Borough Council.

Figure 6.19 Pavement cafés at the southern end of the High Street. (The dominant office building dates from the late 1960s). *Source:* Tony Hall.

This was not so much a direct consequence of planning policy but more as its indirect influence. The cumulative effect of the physical improvements described in this chapter encouraged this trend. The increased number of people living in the centre, a process described in Chapter 7, brought with it a demand for a more sophisticated lifestyle. Moreover, the general corporate stance of the Borough Council, expressed through its regulatory activities, gave an overall encouragement to this particular outward expression of increased business confidence.

The regeneration of the West End

Problems and opportunities

The 'West End' of the Chelmsford Central area, shown in aerial view by Figure 6.20, had, for over 20 years, been perceived as potentially important to the town but by the mid-1980s had become problematic, both physically and economically. An area of unrealised potential, its importance stemmed from its land uses shown by the map in Figure 6.21. It contained the railway station and bus station that were essential transport nodes serving the whole Borough and beyond. They had the advantage not only of being within the central area but also adjacent to each other and, unlike in many towns, on the edge of the principal shopping area. A street view of the main road, Duke Street, looking towards the

Figure 6.20   An aerial view of the West End. *Source:* Peter Rodgers.

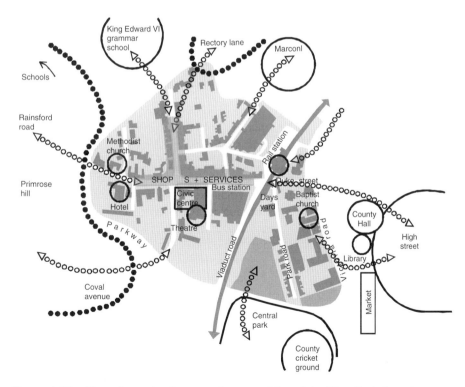

Figure 6.21   The primary land uses and connectivity of the West End. See also Plate 6.1. Reproduced with the permission of Chelmsford Borough Council and the Ordnance Survey on behalf of HMSO. © Crown Copyright 2007. All rights reserved. Licenced number 100046642.

Figure 6.22 Duke Street looking towards railway station. The buildings on the left form the southern edge of the conservation area. The bus station is to the right of the picture. *Source:* Tony Hall.

station is shown in Figure 6.22. The bus station is located to the right of the view, with the railway station on a viaduct in the background. The Civic Centre, containing the Borough Council offices and two theatres, was also located within the West End. The theatres provided the principal concentration of performing arts facilities within the town. It had also been the location of one of the principal campuses of the university, and its predecessor institutions, which had occupied most of the land to the east of the railway line and to the south of Duke Street. Since the late 1980s, it had been the intention to relocate these activities to a new campus on the northern edge of town centre.

The principal cause for concern had been the decline in the West End's retail function. Since the 1980s, the centre of gravity of shopping activity within the town centre had been moving eastwards, leading to a decline in the West End. During the late 1980s and early 1990s, the hope had been that the shopping function would be replaced by a commercial one, with the space left by declining uses providing room to meet a continuing demand for large office blocks. A derelict dairy site on the south side of Parkway had planning permission for a very large office complex in the form of two large structures. Permission had also been given for the replacement of the bus station by an office block and the bus company had sold the site to a commercial developer. Had this come to pass, it would have had disastrous consequences for public transport provision in the town. However, by the mid-1990s nothing had happened because of a decline in the market for large purpose-built office blocks for single users. The only one that did get built in the early 1990s was one for the Sun Life Assurance Company. This also resulted in the loss of one of the major buildings by Chelmsford's 19th-century architect and mayor, Frederick Chancellor. This was to be the last of such significant losses of heritage in Chelmsford.

In 1985, the final section of the inner relief road, Parkway, had opened. This road had had the deleterious effect of severing the West End from its hinterland and creating a 'shatter-zone' of cleared sites, bisected by the road, that were now used as surface car parks. On the other hand, it created an opportunity by removing nearly all the through-traffic from the West End. This could have enabled a re-allocation of road space in favour of the pedestrian, facilitating a general increase in the quality of the public realm, but unfortunately, nothing was to happen at all to the road layout within the West End for the next 20 years.

By the mid-1990s, the bus station and university sites were in poor repair because of the lack of a long-term future. The generally low level of economic activity and poor standard of public environment was causing public concern and pressure from councillors for something to be done. However, matters then started to improve. The area to the north of the main road, Duke Street, had been designated a conservation area back in 1982. The terrace of buildings shown in Figure 6.22 formed its southern edge. Although this was to prove a useful decision, it was a brave one at the time as neither the buildings nor the townscape appeared of outstanding quality. It was the potential townscape quality that had been correctly ascertained. In 1993, the small Co-op supermarket in Duke Street within the terrace of buildings shown in Figure 6.22 had been rebuilt in a style matching the late 19th-century and early-20th-century context of the adjacent buildings. The railway station, and its adjacent multi-storey car park, had been rebuilt in the late 1980s. First Group, the operators of the bus services, bought back the bus station from the property developers who had been unsuccessfully pursuing office uses for its site. The development of a new site for the university meant that the redevelopment of its West End site would definitely occur in the medium term. There was now greater interest from developers in meeting the demand for flats in the area and from smaller enterprises responding to the need for restaurants, take-away outlets and other services.

The West End master plan

In 1998, the Council resolved to undertake a comprehensive public consultation exercise leading to the preparation of a master plan for the whole area. The idea was that a document would be produced that would provide a strategy on which site-specific briefs and other planning guidance would be based.

The forum was open to all – residents, businesses, transport providers, users of shops, transport, car parks and services, churches, arts groups and Borough councillors, as equal participants. The local stakeholders ranged over a fairly small resident population, a network of small and medium businesses, a number of major companies and institutions, several voluntary sector organisations and the public transport operators. There was also a wider public interest in using

West End services, especially the transport users. The exercise was structured around working groups of stakeholders for a range of topics, each chaired by a layperson. The urban design officers of the council also had significant ideas to introduce into the debate, particularly on a new pattern of pedestrian circulation and spaces within the area.

The discussions were wide-ranging and constructive, resulting in a convergence of views in to a vision of the future form and function of the West End. Agreement was reached on all topics except traffic circulation. Here there was such a strong difference of opinion, particularly about whether cars should be barred from Duke Street, opposite the bus station, that this matter had to be left for resolution at a later date.

The new vision centred on the amplification of the existing arts role of the area with renewed emphasis on the visual and performing arts. Retail premises would focus on providing services especially for the daytime office users. The land uses were to be mixed and include residential, retail and small office elements. The most imaginative outcome of the master plan process was a proposed reconfiguration of pedestrian spaces and circulation as shown in Figure 6.23. The area of the public park between the university site and the railway viaduct, owned by the Borough Council, would be relocated to the centre of the redeveloped university site, while maintaining pedestrian access to both Central Park, the railway station and Essex County Hall. This new space would be connected by a new pedestrian access under the railway viaduct to the site of the redeveloped bus station. As part of the bus station redevelopment, a new urban pedestrian space would be created and this new route would connect to it. This new space would, in turn, have access to the Civic Centre and its theatres.

The master plan was approved by the council in March 2000 (CBC, 2000a). This was followed by the approval of site-specific briefs for the bus station site (CBC, 2000b) and the former University site (CBC, 2001d).

The redevelopment of the bus station

The benefits of a redevelopment of the bus station site had been clear to all interested parties ever since First Group had reclaimed it from the office developers, and they were expressed in the planning brief (CBC, 2000b). They were dependent on the removal of maintenance activities to a new bus-servicing depot in the south of the town that would then facilitate

- a small bus station, with a 'teardrop'-shaped circulation layout, on the existing site;
- redevelopment of the rest of the site.

To these had to be added the following objectives of the West End master plan:

- mixed uses;
- the new pattern of urban spaces and pedestrian circulation.

Unfortunately, there was considerable delay in the progress of the development because of financial and political issues within First Group. Establishing the new service and maintenance depot, on an industrial estate in the south of

Figure 6.23 An extract from the West End master plan (CBC, 2000a) showing the proposed reconfiguration of pedestrian spaces. See also Plate 6.2. Reproduced with the permission of Chelmsford Borough Council and the Ordnance Survey on behalf of HMSO. © Crown Copyright 2007. All rights reserved. Licence number 100046642.

the urban area, went ahead. The matter of the bus station site, though, became subject to protracted negotiations between First Group, the Borough officers and, latter, the Essex County Council officers. Agreement was not reached until 2002 and building did not start until the end of 2004. The essentials of the strategy for the site were

- a new bus station paid for, and ultimately to be owned by, Essex County Council;
- a new public square linked through the arches of the railway viaduct to the former university site;
- ground floor shops;
- flats in a tower above the shops.

Figure 6.24 A computer generated image of the Bus Station redevelopment.
Source: Barratt (Eastern Counties).

The negotiated scheme placed a four-storey building in an arc around the new bus station, giving a strong street edge, together with a residential tower next to a new square. Shops were provided at ground level fronting both the street and the bus station. The 170 dwellings were accommodated both in the tower and above the shops. The large open area of the bus circulation loop was complemented by the crescent-shaped architecture and four-storey scale. An important requirement, which was handled successfully, was the provision of communal private open space. This was provided at a higher level over the top of the shops. Figure 6.24 shows a view of the bus station fronting Duke Street with the residential tower behind. The residential component of the scheme was undertaken by Barratt.

What was missing from all this was any office uses. The problem was not that there was a demand for new office blocks – there was not – but that more people living in the town centre would create a demand for more legal, financial and other services. These would need somewhere to go. Unfortunately, because of the difficult circumstances surrounding the particular history of the development of this site, their provision could not be secured. Nevertheless, the appearance of the new structures was a striking and modern contribution to legibility and a sense of place in this central location. If there was a location in the centre where a tower, and modern styling, was appropriate then this was the place.

The former university site

Along with the bus station, the university campus in Victoria Road South was one of the two most important development sites, not just within the West End, but the town as a whole. It had a very substantial area of over 4 ha and was adjacent to the railway station on its north side and the Essex County Hall on its east side. Not only was it large, visually prominent and central, it had a key role to play in the establishment of the new pedestrian routes and spaces that were a key, and imaginative, part of the West End strategy.

The site had had a long history as a centre of community and educational activities in the town. It had been the location of the art school and principal library, established 100 years earlier in an imposing building designed by Frederick Chancellor, Chelmsford's 19th-century mayor and architect. Subsequently a technical school and technical college found their home on the site. In the latter part of the 20th century, it became the location of a higher education college that was transmuted in to a polytechnic and subsequently became part of what is now Anglia Ruskin University.

When the construction of a new university campus on the north side of the town centre began in the early 1990s, it was clear that the availability of the Victoria Road site for redevelopment was only a matter of time. Although this time period might be 10 years or more and occurring in stages, it would happen eventually. It was important that a detailed brief for the site was approved within the context of the West End master plan. The first draft was considered by the Borough councillors early in 2001. The key elements were the introduction of arts uses, and the rearrangement of public space and routes, as required by the master plan. An area of the public park owned by the Borough Council was to be reallocated to the centre of the site and connected through under the arches of the railway viaduct to the bus station site as shown in Figure 6.23. The councillors added three important concerns of their own – that certain specific trees, including a magnolia, should be retained and that the old Library and Art School building should be retained and that the adjacent conservation area should be extended to give the Borough Council control over these matters. This building was important in terms of Chelmsford's history, and formed an important component of the street scene in Victoria Road South but, unfortunately, had been refused listing by English Heritage. There was no question that the one listed building on the site, the former Quaker Meeting House, a very prominent and handsome structure, would be retained and reused. The report supporting the case for the extension of the conservation area was undertaken by the county council on behalf of the Borough Council and the extension to the conservation area was approved late in 2001. The brief (CBC, 2001d) was approved by the Borough Council in April 2001.

The university agreed in the same year to sell the site to Countryside Properties in stages, as teaching activities moved out. Countryside Properties put together a team consisting of a number of firms, covering the range of professional skills required and including the Richard Rogers Partnership. In September 2002, they came forward with an application for outline planning permission supported by a fairly detailed scheme for the redevelopment of the site. The scheme had a strong urban form rising to nine storeys producing a density of over 300 dph. It contained a new and dramatic proposal, a 'green bridge' forming a pedestrian link between Central Park and the relocated green space in the centre of the site.

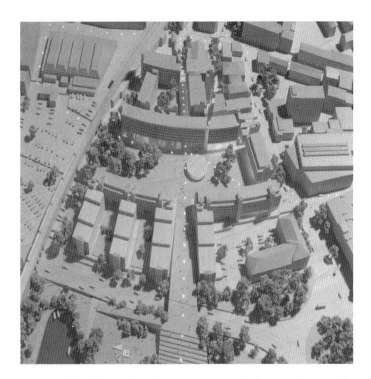

Figure 6.25 A model of the redevelopment proposals for the former university site. *Source:* The Richard Rodgers Partnership.

This bridge would span Parkway and be planted with grass to a width of 20–30 m. The proposals were illustrated by a model as shown in Figure 6.25. Although predominantly residential, the scheme was a mixed-use one. It included significant arts uses around the green space and commercial and retail uses towards the railway station. The central green area was arranged to provide a strong east–west link between the bus station and the Essex County Hall and retained all the significant trees within it. Frederick Chancellor's Library and Art School would be used for the visual arts. Other art activities, especially dance, would also surround the green space, allowing activities to spill out on to it.

When it came to consideration by the planning committee, the concept as a whole, especially the 'green bridge', was greatly welcomed. Not only did it comply with the Council's strategy and detailed brief, but it had interpreted them in a positive and imaginative way. There were only two points of contention. The first was the retention of teaching Building, dating from the early 1930s, which had a significant stair tower and glazed roof over an internal courtyard. Countryside Properties had originally intended to retain it, but later proposed demolition to make way for a new building for Essex Dance. Conditions were applied requiring specific architectural salvage. The other issue was the use of the listed, former Quaker Meeting House. The developer suggested retail, but the committee were interest in retaining its fine uninterrupted internal space for arts and community use and possibly trade exhibitions, and this was included in the a conditions on the planning permission.

The new university campus

The higher education institutions in Chelmsford that preceded the formation of Anglia Ruskin University had long planned for a new campus, either by extending and rebuilding at the central site in the West End or at a new site on the edge of town. Following achievement of polytechnic status in 1990, additional funding became available from the government. Expansion was planned and a new site needed to be developed to take advantage of it. A disused former ball-bearing factory was acquired for the purpose. The site had the advantage of an ample supply of land in a potentially attractive location by the river while, at that same time, being conveniently located on the northern edge of the town centre. The principal challenge of the site to the university was the cost of decontamination. Although such a site would later be seen as exemplifying 'brownfield' development and promoting employment at all salary levels, at the time the Essex County Council saw it as representing a loss of employment land because of the replacement of manufacturing use by one of services.

A master plan for the site was prepared by the then polytechnic's agents at the time and agreed with the Borough Council. A central feature at the southern end of the site was a major building to house the library, with two wings spreading out from it on either side to accommodate teaching functions. Nearby would be new student residences. Further buildings would then extend north as the institution expanded.

The site was ideal, and the idea of northward expansion along the river was an attractive one that would continue to be pursued over time. Unfortunately, implementation of the master plan was characterised in its early days by a lack of firm control, although this situation was, later, to be decisively reversed. The early 1990s was not a period when the Borough Council was intervening proactively with detailed briefs. For its part, the polytechnic, later university, had recently privatised its estate functions and hoped it could get by without a client side, or a director of estates. The new library building, now known as the Queen's Building, shown in Figure 6.26, was handled by a design-and-build process. It was not of particularly distinguished appearance but negotiations with the Borough officers did ensure that it neatly closed the perspective of the view down New Street. Adjoining it was a particularly unfortunate piece of dual-carriageway road, totally over-engineered for its purpose and obstructing, rather than encouraging, pedestrian movement.

There was, however, one very significant achievement from this period. Members of the academic staff had pointed out that if the new buildings were of low-energy design, and if their performance was monitored as a piece of research, then the European Union grants could be forthcoming. This idea was taken up for the Queen's Building, and all subsequent teaching buildings. It is now one of the most important features of the new campus.

The student residences, illustrated in Figure 6.27, were built by Countryside Properties at the same time as the Queen's Building. They were of pleasant appearance but, unfortunately, did not incorporate the same imaginative low-energy design.

Figure 6.26 The new University campus – the first major new low-energy building, the Queen's Building containing the university library. *Source:* Anglia Ruskin University.

Following its experience with the first phase of construction, the former poly-technic, now university, had a change of heart. It created an estates office to manage development of its new campus and act as a client side for dealing with contractors and developers. It resolved to commission quality architecture, a goal desired by the Borough's officers. The first fruit of this change was the building known as Rivermead Gate, constructed in 1996 and illustrated by Figure 6.28. Although in style it mirrored, rather than competed with, the adjacent Queen's Building, it was a step forward in several important respects. It was a mixed-use concept with rents from retailing on the ground floor financing a building that contained a doctor's surgery on the first floor and university offices above that. The retail uses also provided a frontage to the public street and to the public areas of the university campus. The design was by a local firm, David Ruffle Architects.

The next building was the campus's first major teaching building, the Sawyers Building, shown in Figure 6.29. It was a low-energy building embodying one of the two wings that the original master plan envisaged either side of the library. However, it was expressed in a more contemporary architectural language than the library. Its alignment also enabled the process of opening up the river bank to begin in earnest. A footpath and places for eating out were provided on the university side of the river. As a condition of planning permission, the university was required to provide a new pedestrian and cycle bridge linking the campus with the parkland and pedestrian cycle way on the other side of the river owned by the Borough Council. The campus was being physically integrated into one of the town's 'green wedges'.

Figure 6.27 The new University campus – the student residences. *Source:* Anglia Ruskin University.

The entire process moved up a gear with the commissioning of a design for the next structure to be built, the new Ashcroft Business School. Lord Ashcroft, the Conservative Party treasurer, and later chancellor of the university, had made a very generous offer for funding of a purpose-designed building for the university's business school. The building would form the wing on the other side of the Queen's Building to the Sawyers Building but not necessarily in an identical style. The university decided to make the design the subject of an architectural competition. The low-energy building policy would be maintained.

Figure 6.28 The new university campus – Rivermead Gate, a mixed-use building with shops on the ground floor, a doctor's surgery on the first floor and university offices above. *Source:* Anglia Ruskin University.

Figure 6.29 The new university campus – the first major new low-energy teaching building, the Sawyers Building. *Source:* Anglia Ruskin University.

Figure 6.30 The new university campus – the Ashcroft Building, by Wilkinson Eyre, containing the business school. *Source:* Anglia Ruskin University.

A lay panel, which included one Borough councillor, was set up to judge the entries. The winner was Wilkinson Eyre Architects with a design in a very contemporary style, making extensive use of glass cladding, as shown by Figure 6.30. There was little problem in obtaining planning consent as not only was the design clearly of high quality but the architectural language was appropriate to its context, in this case a new university in a modern expanding town.

So impressed was the university with the design of the new business school that it commissioned Wilkinson Eyre to work on a revised master plan for the campus. By this time, the 1990s version was badly in need of review. The new plan incorporated an amended circulation pattern, with buildings arranged along a pedestrian way, following the northward line of the river. The short dual carriageway at the southern entrance to the campus was to be replaced by a pedestrian space with a vehicle access to the site coming only from the north. The style of the Ashcroft Building now became the theme for the whole of the rest of the campus. A new master plan was approved by the Borough Council in 2002.

Chapter 7

Living in the centre

Before 1995, there was little evidence in Chelmsford of the repopulation of the town centre that was to become such a prominent feature by 2000. Developers showed little or no interest in residential uses, preferring to seek permission for new office and retail blocks. Chelmsford's 1991–2001 Borough plan (CBC, 1997a) made no provision for new dwellings in the town centre but, on the contrary, reserved former industrial land for 'employment uses', following the lead of the Essex County structure plan (ECC, 1991, 1995). This issue is discussed in more generally on page 9 of the Introduction.

There was, however, potential for town-centre living, even if not fully understood by all at the time. The railway station was situated in the town centre and offered frequent services to central London, just over 30 min away. It had a concentration of employment in retailing, public administration, financial services and higher education. There were ample amounts of brownfield land, much of it in the ownership of the Borough Council and, somewhat ironically, preserved from development by the Borough and County Council policies. There was the potential for the significant urban renaissance described in Chapter 6.

The first examples of change

Durrant Court and Ashby House

The first significant example of the provision of town-centre flats occurred in 1995 with the conversion of what was then know as Globe House, shown in Figure 7.1. Globe House was a former industrial building, a flatted factory on four floors, in New Street, on the northern edge of the town centre. It had originally formed part of the former now defunct ball-bearing factory that had now become the new site for the main campus of the university.

The development was a mixed-use one, incorporating a fitness centre on the ground floor of the main building, now known as Durrant Court, with flats above. At the rear was an office wing, now called Ashby House. It was not proposed for

Figure 7.1 Durrant Court and Ashby House, New Street, a former industrial building converted to residential and office uses. *Source:* Chelmsford Borough Council.

residential use because it was affected by industrial noise from an adjacent flour mill. It should be noted in passing that this was an example of the problems of the transition from industrial to residential uses in inner-city areas. The remaining, but long-standing, industrial activities have the potential to cause nuisance to the incoming residents and become a source of conflict.

Had this conversion occurred in the centre of, say, London or Manchester, or had it taken place in Chelmsford 10 years later, its high ceilings and extensive floor areas would have lent itself to loft-style apartments, spacious and for higher-income groups. As it happened, artificial low ceilings were inserted and small one- and two-bedroom single-aspect flats were created, half of them north-facing and half of them south-facing.

The developers had also acquired land to the south of the building. They included in the planning application a low-intensity use in the shape of a small supermarket and car park with no active frontage to New Street. Against the recommendation of the officers at the time, the planning committee refused to accept this. It was agreed that this part of the application would be reserved for later decision so that the flats could proceed. This part of the site subsequently became the Atlantic Hotel, a development discussed at the end of this chapter on page 169. This decision set out an important marker for future policy. Had such low-intensity, car-based uses, particularly those that did not contribute to a quality townscape, been allowed in the town centre, then the achievement of the urban renaissance described in this and the previous chapter would have been frustrated.

The important positive pointer for the future was, however, the rapid sale of all the flats including the small north-facing ones. This was to be the first revelation of the high degree of untapped residential demand in the town centre.

Corinthian Square

The next example was the development by Barratt, in 1997, of the site adjacent to the Essex County Cricket Ground, a scheme that they later called Corinthian Square. It might have been expected that they would have wanted to take advantage of the views of the cricket that the site would have afforded, given the substantial premium that they could have charged on the price of the flats. They might have had large balconies overlooking the play as, for example, at the Sussex County Cricket Ground in Hove. Unfortunately, this was not to be. Barratt were, at this stage, not in the business of designing for a particular site and wanted only to accommodate their standard dwelling types. The first proposals also paid little regard to the character of the adjacent conservation area for the new London Road. They were considered unacceptable by the Council's development control officers who were now aware of both the design policy issues and the mood of the planning committee. Barratt had, by now, their own direct experience of dealing with the new planning committee (in respect of their Princes Road site, discussed in Chapter 5 on page 87) and agreed to negotiate. The resulting scheme, as shown in Figure 7.2, showed considerable modification of the Barratt standard dwelling-types and was achieved through substantial negotiation with officers. Although not remarkable architecture, the

Figure 7.2 The Corinthian Square development overlooking the Essex County cricket ground. *Source:* Paul Starr.

materials and roof shapes took account of the local context and the principal windows afforded some view of the cricket. Barratt opened a temporary sales office on the site and sold all of the flats before construction had hardly started. Again, the evidence of untapped demand for town-centre flats was impressive.

The Chelmer Waterside story

At the same time as Corinthian Square was being considered, a far more important part of the story was unfolding within the area that was to become known as Chelmer Waterside. This was an area to the east of the town centre, lying beside and between the River Chelmer and the Chelmer and Blackwater Canal. An aerial view is shown in Figure 7.3. The edge of the town-centre shops can be seen in the top left-hand corner of the picture. The left-hand edge of the picture shows part of the eastern valley 'green wedge,' with its footpaths and cycle ways, as described in Chapter 6, page 125. The land between the river and canal had once been the site of the town's gasworks, and at its western end two gasholders remain in operation. The rest of the gasworks site was acquired by the Borough Council and used mainly for surface car parking. Later policies were to propose the regeneration of the entire Chelmer Waterside area through mixed-use development. However, this was far from the case in 1995.

Figure 7.3   An aerial view of Chelmer Waterside. The river Chelmer can be seen on the left of the picture and the canal basin is to the right. See also Plate 7.1. *Source:* Peter Rodgers.

Apart from a functioning woodyard, the canal basin was surrounded by derelict warehouses which were not only unsightly but obscured the view of the water. It was common to find that the residents of the town were unaware of the existence of the canal basin. The town turned its back on this historic asset. The gasholders were to the south side of the basin and, to the west, were the rear parking and servicing for town-centre shops.

The locks and waterway of the canal, including the basin, but not the adjacent buildings, had been restored in 1993 in a partnership between the canal owners, the Inland Waterways Association, the Essex County Council and the Borough Council. Although a brief for the canal basin (CBC, 1994) had been prepared, officers had found it difficult to interest developers. It must be remembered that this was shortly before the government's promotion of 'brownfield' development and shortly before the evidence of the high degree of demand for town-centre flats in Chelmsford became manifest. Volume house builders generally based their business plans on what they had sold before and did not undertake the research that would have revealed the size and nature of the new markets.

Coate's Quay – Phase 1

In 1997, the house-building firm Higgins agreed to have a go at one corner of the Basin, known as Coate's Quay. The scheme comprised 41 flats at a density of 44 per hectare. As at the cricket ground site, these were the house builder's standard dwelling-types, in this case blocks of flats with a T-shaped plan. Great efforts were made by officers in negotiation to achieve sympathetic roof shapes and building materials, in this case brick and slate in keeping with the historic period of the canal basin. The stylistic rationale was that, in addition to canal itself, there were some period buildings that would be advantageous to retain for the new development to be in sympathy with. An existing house was retained and incorporated in the scheme. The view of the completed scheme from the canal basin is shown in Figure 7.4. Although a degree of active frontage was obtained along the canal basin and the northern edge of the site, the western edge was, unfortunately, given a blank wall protecting communal private space. The prominent corner between them was addressed by bathroom windows and protected by bushes at ground level. This sort of result would never have been permitted if it had been proposed a few years later, but at the time, officers were only too glad for a developer to agree to take on the project and agree to some measure of aesthetic control. The remarkable outcome of this scheme was that all the flats sold instantly, much to the surprise of Higgins and to the gratification of the Council and its officers.

The Waterfront Place restaurant

A local entrepreneur specialising in restaurants now came forward and offered to build an entirely new and substantial restaurant on the opposite bank of the canal in the first phase of the Coate's Quay scheme. Although of modern construction, the new restaurant, illustrated by Figure 7.5, had a sympathetic roof shape and materials and incorporated an existing industrial building for use as banqueting facilities. The proposal also made full use of its water frontage and

Figure 7.4   Coate's Quay – Phase 1. *Source:* Roy Chandler.

Figure 7.5   Waterfront Place restaurant and Coate's Quay – Phase 2. *Source:* Chelmsford Borough Council.

opened up a path along the canal bank. The planning application was readily agreed to. In spite of its still insalubrious surroundings, the restaurant, called Waterfront Place, proved an outstanding success and further demonstrated what could be achieved through development in this type of location.

Coate's Quay – Phase 2

Buoyed by the success of the sales of its first flat development on the canal, at Coate's Quay, Higgins embarked upon a second phase, which was to represent a decisive step forward in the way such development was carried out. This was to be an architect-designed, mixed-use scheme tailored to the site. The land in question was that between the first scheme and the Waterfront Place restaurant. There was again a very substantial amount for successful negotiation, but this time it was pitched at a much more sophisticated level, in light of both the emerging policy framework and the successful sale of the previous scheme. The resulting scheme, comprising 13 flats and 4 shops, was by David Wood Architects and is illustrated in Figure 7.6. It shared with the previous scheme the theme of the 19th century dockland aesthetic in terms of materials and roof shapes. The significant improvements were

- active frontages to all public roads;
- ground floor retail units providing a mix of uses;
- larger windows, some with balconies, giving views of the canal;
- pedestrian access to the waterside;

Figure 7.6   Coate's Quay – Phase 2. See also Plate 7.2. *Source:* Roy Chandler.

- buildings wrapped round the canal basin with continuous shallow-plan form;
- a new office for the canal company, weather-boarded in a neovernacular style.

The Chelmer Waterside strategy

As the canal-related developments proceeded, their very success drew attention to the need for a comprehensive strategy for the whole Chelmer Waterside area, of which the canal basin was a part, and for site-specific briefs for its component parts. The regeneration of the whole area was now central to council policy. Chelmsford was fortunate in having such a large area of potential developable brownfield land so close to its centre. Not only that, the manner in which both a river and canal flowed through it created the potential for attractive riverside development. A substantial area was owned by the Borough Council and used as surface car parking. Another significant segment was that owned by successor companies to British Gas and possessed considerable potential that could be realised if the gasholders could be relocated. Other small parcels of land were occupied by smaller, low-intensity businesses, such as scrapyards and woodyards, that would have every incentive to relocate when land values rose as a consequence of regeneration. A separate brief for the gasholder site had already been approved (CBC, 1999b). In 2000, the Council approved for consultation an overall strategy prepared by its urban design officers for the whole Waterside area. It set out the general planning policy, especially with regard to access by all modes and the constraints posed by flood prevention works and underground services crossing the site. The strategy area was divided into nine parts with the intention that a more detailed brief would be prepared for each one. Also in 2000, the consultation versions of briefs for the land west of the canal, north-east of the canal and the 'peninsula site', between the river and canal, were published. A consultation brief was subsequently published for the land between Parkway and the river. These briefs were used in negotiations with prospective developers immediately. These could be seen, in effect, as part of the consultation process. Following this extended period of consultation and negotiation, final approval by the Council of the Chelmer Waterside Strategy as supplementary planning guidance was given 2 years later (CBC, 2002c).

Lockside Marina

Higgins subsequently acquired a scrap metal yard at the other end of the canal basin near its entrance lock. This site fell within the coverage of a very detailed brief for the land north east of the canal (CBC, 2002d). The brief both helped to unlock the site and direct the shape of development. It contained a diagrammatic plan shown in Figure 7.7 with a shallow plan-block curving in a semicircle around a new marina. Far from feeling constrained by such prescription, the developers copied it, as can be seen from the aerial view of the completed scheme in Figure 7.8. The new block, shown in Figures 7.8 and 7.9, was designed for the site by David Wood Architects, who had been responsible for Coate's Quay phase 2. While a style reflecting the canal's 19th century context was

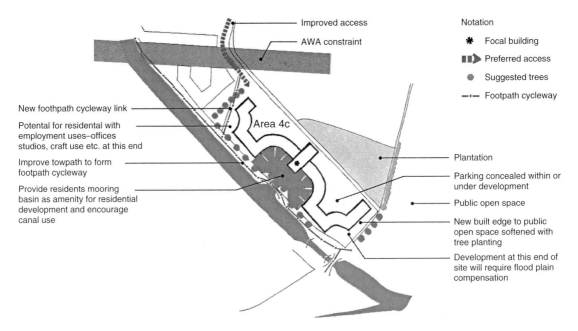

Notation

✳ Focal building

▮▮▷ Preferred access

● Suggested trees

—•— Footpath cycleway

Improved access

AWA constraint

New foothpath cycleway link

Potential for residential with employment uses–offices studios, craft use etc. at this end

Area 4c

Improve towpath to form footpath cycleway

Provide residents mooring basin as amenity for residential development and encourage canal use

Plantation

Parking concealed within or under development

Public open space

New built edge to public open space softened with tree planting

Development at this end of site will require flood plain compensation

Figure 7.7   An extract from a planning brief (CBC, 2002d) proposing suggestions the site of the Lockside Marina development. Reproduced with the permission of the Ordnance Survey on behalf of HMSO. © Crown copyright 2007. All rights reserved. Licence number 100046642.

Figure 7.8   An aerial view of Lockside Marina as completed. *Source:* Peter Rodgers.

Figure 7.9 A canal-side view of Lockside Marina as completed. *Source:* Chelmsford Borough Council.

encouraged at the head of the canal basin, as one moved down it, and the context changed, a more contemporary approach was considered appropriate as no existing buildings were being retained.

The scheme incorporated 106 flats, at a density of 160 dph, with 25% affordable housing. It showed the following advances on Higgins' previous canal-side developments at Coate's Quay:

- larger dwelling sizes including two three-bedroom and two duplex flats;
- larger windows over looking the canal;
- larger balconies giving significant private open space to each flat.

The building took full advantage of its site and connected well into the footpath and cycle network. Although confined to one wing, the social-rented accommodation was not distinguishable from the outside and offered a high standard of amenity.

Planning permission was readily granted at the end of 2000, although construction was delayed and the first stage was not completed until early 2002. The sales office was opened well in advance of completion. For the first release, prospective buyers camped out for 24 h in advance and all flats were sold within 40 min. For the second release, queuing started at 6 a.m. and most were sold within 40 min of opening. The subsequent stages sold almost as quickly.

Readers may find the scene shown in Figures 7.8 and 7.9 to be rather pastoral for a town-centre location. This was the effect of the 'green wedge' policy, which brought the countryside down the river valleys all the way to the town centre, as described in Chapter 6, page 125. The footpath and cycle way for the eastern valley connected Lockside Marina to the town centre.

From the author's personal experience as a one-time resident of the block, the partial enclosure of the marina by the block and the large windows to the flats produced a communal feeling for the residents and made it a remarkably pleasant place to live in. The footpath and cycle way connection to the town centre was convenient and well used.

Another developer follows suit

The success of Higgins' second and third canal-side residential developments set the tone, and gave a lead, for all subsequent town-centre schemes. It had been clearly demonstrated that there was substantial, if not overwhelming, demand for town-centre flats and that architect-designed schemes, tailored to the site and offering a high standard of accommodation, could be more profitable than developments consisting of standard types. Other developers now followed suit – most notably Barratt, a firm not previously known for this type of scheme.

Wells Street

Barratt had previously acquired a small site at Wells Street in the heart of the town centre, near the bus and railway stations. This was a tight site, a former private car park in street of some character. The design went through a prolonged negotiation starting with an initial proposal that left a large gap in

Figure 7.10 The Wells Street mixed-use development in the West End. *Source:* Chelmsford Borough Council.

the street, had a dead street frontage, an angular corner and unruly roof form. The final scheme strengthened the continuity of the street, shopfronts along the ground floor, a curved corner flowing with the street line and a rhythmic elevational composition. It was a mixed-use scheme with the ground floor entirely non-residential and occupied by offices and one shop and with flats above. One parking space per flat and no garden space were accepted as a reasonable trade-off for mixed use and close proximity to transport. The scheme as built, shown in Figure 7.10, contributed to character of the conservation area. Intensive and positive negotiation by officers had produced a scheme that integrated well into the street scene and provided new shops at street level.

Capital Square

Barratt now embarked upon two substantial mixed-use schemes, both architect-designed for the site and incorporating 25% affordable housing.

The first was on a site in Victoria Road, on the northern edge of the town centre. This was a key site for regeneration in the town centre and was the subject of a detailed design brief (CBC, 2002e). An extract showing the block layout

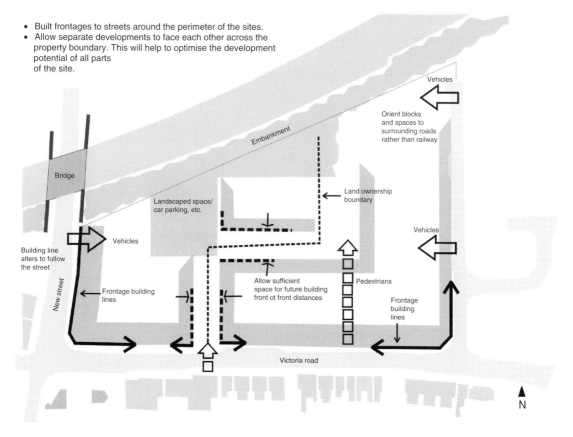

Figure 7.11 The diagram from planning brief (CBC, 2002e) for the site of Capital Square development showing the desired arrangement of blocks, frontages and open space. See also plate 7.3.
Source: Chelmsford Borough Council.

Figure 7.12 A street view of the Capital Square development by Barratt. *Source:* Tony Hall.

Figure 7.13 The rear court giving service access to the Capital Square shops and flats. *Source:* Chelmsford Borough Council.

principles is shown in Figure 7.11. Part of the site was a post office sorting office, which, it was hoped, would eventually have to come available for re-development but had so far failed to do so. Almost half the area, though, had long been disused and was acquired by Barratt for a mixed-use scheme of 4 shops and 108 flats. Guided by the brief and negotiation with officers, this scheme shown in Figures 7.12–7.14 was completed in 2005 and was designed by PRP Architects. Figure 7.12 shows the view of the development from the street. Figure 7.13 shows the rear court, which gave service access to the shops and flats. Figure 7.14 shows the separate block of flats to the rear of the site. Although there were some balconies, there was a trade-off between a central location and the extent of private amenity space. The constraints of the central location resulted in

- flats that were not large;
- a limited amount of communal space;
- 80% parking;
- shops serviced from the front.

The important point was, however, the way a mixed-use scheme at a residential density of 120 dph had been successfully integrated into the urban townscape.

Figure 7.14 The flats along the northern edge of the Capital Square development. *Source:* Chelmsford Borough Council.

Callow Court

The true example of Barratt's emulation of the success of Higgins' third canal-side scheme was their redevelopment of the former site of the Chelmsford Bowls Club. Although approximately north-facing, the site had the advantage of extensive views over Central Park. The design, by the Omega Partnership, incorporated fairly large flats with balconies and large windows, taking full advantage of the views, as can be seen from Figure 7.15. The penthouse flat was redolent of the 1930s art deco 'ocean liner' style. Overall, the appearance was distinctive, contributing to a sense of place. It was completed in 2004.

A new New Street

The Capital Square scheme formed an important corner on New Street. New Street linked the new university campus, described in Chapter 6, page 149, to the town centre and was the subject of significant changes. Up until the early 1980s, it had been a predominantly industrial area, the site not only of the ball-bearing factory but also the historic Marconi works and a large warehouse from the early 1970s. The Marconi works were the world's first purpose-built electronics factory and its original office block is now, fortunately, a listed building.

Figure 7.15 The Callow Court flats by Barratt overlooking the Central Park. *Source:* Tony Hall.

There was also a parade of shops from the 1950s, serving some side streets of 19th-century terraced housing. The decline of manufacturing industry had released a large amount of brownfield land. The official policy of both Essex County Council and Chelmsford Borough Council during the late 1980s and early 1990s had been that this should remain as industrial land. However, not only did industry not return, but a new university campus, far more typical of the post-industrial economy, had moved in. With the conversion of the former industrial building, then known as Globe House, to flats and offices, as described on page 154, the whole area was clearly set to change in a different direction.

The refusal of the planning committee to sanction a low-intensity use in the form of a supermarket, described on page 155, as part of the Globe House (now Durrant and Ashby House) redevelopment created an opportunity for a local entrepreneur. He built hotels, something Chelmsford was very short of, and proposed one for this site. The Atlantic Hotel, as it became known, received planning permission, and was constructed, in 1997. It is illustrated in Figure 7.16. Although it was a significant improvement in terms of use and design on past proposals for edge of centre sites in Chelmsford, the commercial attitudes and planning policies regarding car use that applied at the time meant that it did

Figure 7.16   The Atlantic Hotel in New Street. *Source:* Chelmsford Borough Council.

Figure 7.17 Mixed-use development in New Street opposite the University and Durrant House. *Source:* Tony Hall.

Figure 7.18 The mixed-use development in New Street showing relationship to a side street. *Source:* Chelmsford Borough Council.

not meet the design outcomes that would have been expected 5 years later. The Borough Council's car parking standards required a minimum number of spaces for hotel rooms and the need to accommodate the required amount of parking restricted the size of hotel that could be constructed. Furthermore, the commercial perception was that patrons would only come if there was ample parking and that this had to be in front so that they could see it. Although the building faced the road, most of it was set back behind the car park with a loss of direct frontage and the chance to create the feeling of a proper street.

As matters turned out, the amount and location of car parking did not prove commercially essential because of the hotel's central location and a continued shortage of rooms in Chelmsford. The parking policies were eventually changed to restrict, rather than require, parking for town-centre commercial uses, in line with central government policy. Furthermore, the hotel restaurant was set up as a separate commercial undertaking, seeking custom from non-residents. As it was at the rear of the building, a sign had to be erected in New Street informing passers-by that there was a actually a restaurant there. Clearly, had the restaurant been located with street frontage this would have been greatly to its commercial advantage.

In 1997, the decision was taken to build on the car park to create new shops with flats above fronting directly onto the street and with much greater height. Permission was granted readily, although construction was delayed. The difference in the physical form as a result of changing attitudes and policy was very marked.

In 1997, other planning applications came in for shops with flats above for two sites on the opposite side of the road, and with a very similar appearance to, those proposed for the Atlantic Hotel site. They were constructed by 2004 and are shown in Figure 7.17. Figure 7.18 illustrates how they were integrated with the two-storey 19th-century terraced house in the adjacent side street. Attention to matters such as this is what a proactive approach to urban design must be about. This development represented a definite change for New Street not only to its physical appearance but also to the intensity and nature of its land use, a process that was now set to continue.

Conclusion

Results on the ground

Part Two of this book described the redevelopment of Chelmsford at the turn of the millennium, setting out both its origins and outcomes. The challenge of guiding this redevelopment provided the basis for the pragmatic evolution of the proactive approach described in Part One. What was achieved on the ground was the result of this approach. Inevitably, and correctly, the procedures recommended here will be judged according the quality of their outcomes. Hopefully, readers will use this book as a guide to visit the town and make their own judgements on the spot. What cannot be denied, however, is that there was a dramatic change: the town was turned around in regard to both its physical form and the way that tasks were carried out.

Much of the results of these efforts is still to come. Indeed, what has been started will be an ongoing and self-improving process. Nevertheless, some remarkable changes could already be seen. The most visible consequence to date has been the improvement of the quality of the town centre. The centre of the town is different now from what it was in the 1980s, and earlier, not just in its built form but also in the way it was used by the people. The public realm is now pedestrian-dominated and characterised by pavement cafes and an active nightlife. This lifestyle was not explicitly planned for, as people could not be compelled to be the proprietors or customers of such enterprises. What the planning process did was to provide the context in which it could flourish. Within the town centre it is not just the buildings but also the activities that accompany them and the public spaces that provide the settings for these activities. There is now an air of vibrancy and sophistication in the shops, bars and cafes surrounding the public spaces that give the lie to the old image and jokes about Essex. Architect-designed flats look out over the waterways. New architecture is also prominent in public buildings such as the bus station and the new university campus. Style is based on historic or modern themes as appropriate to the context. Moving away from the town centre to the suburbs, new development is in the form of houses and gardens reflecting the urban approach of the *Essex design guide* (EPOA, 1997). The new suburban housing is at higher density, 30–35 dph, than in the past but, nevertheless, exhibits an urban streetscape in distinctive local styles. The cars are parked behind the frontage. Biodiversity is encouraged and back gardens provide an outdoor room. The green corridors formed from the river valleys accommodate parkland and well-used pedestrian and cycle ways linking the residential areas to, and through, the town centre.

To what degree was all this merely the result of general economic and demographic changes and of the requirements of central government and County Council policies? Chelmsford had never been within a major growth area, as proposed by national or regional strategies but, nevertheless, had met, and continues to be challenged by, substantial growth targets for new dwellings. Favourable conditions for development and expansion had been present since the 1960s but had not been taken advantage of. The evidence for this is in the buildings of all periods from the early 1970s to the mid-1990s. There is no evidence that, had a change of policy not been made in 1996, this state of affairs would not have continued for many years. This was the case both in many other parts of the country and even in some other parts of Essex. Moreover, change at Chelmsford began before the publication of the revised *Essex design guide* (EPOA, 1997) and before the promotion by the central government of an urban renaissance. Where prior credit must given, though, is to the design team at Essex County Council. Without the publication of the first Essex guide (ECC, 1973), which led to the revised version in 1997, the task of improving quality with Chelmsford Borough would have been immeasurably more difficult.

For Chelmsford in the early 1990s, the idea of an urban renaissance and high-density living was genuinely radical. Notwithstanding this, the Borough Council embraced the challenge of higher densities and high quality and raised the importance of urban design in its working practices. It secured better-quality housing on greenfield and brownfield sites, in numerous schemes, ranging in size between 30 and 500 dwellings. This was achieved by weaving urban design into the planning process, and securing better quality in new development as a result.

What was remarkable at Chelmsford was that the improvements applied to the whole town, and surrounding settlements, and represented a permanent change for the better. A uniformly higher standard of building was being realised, not just trophy architecture or exemplar estates. It was also something that has continued over time. In particular, the processes for achieving quality continued after significant staff and political changes subsequent to the 1996–2003 period.

Some important lessons

More planning means better architecture

What then can be learnt from the way quality was achieved? One of the most significant lessons from the experience at Chelmsford was the way that increasing planning intervention gave scope for more, not less, quality architecture. Over time, there was a steady increase in the quantity, and degree of prescription, of published planning policy relating to design control. Use was made of policy in national guidance, design guides, local plan policy and site-specific briefs. As these became more detailed, clearer and more purposeful, so the quality on the ground improved. Before the introduction of the explicit controls, what was built was the standard developer product with minimal architectural input. With strong planning intervention, architect-designed schemes, tailored to the site, became the norm in the town centre and common elsewhere. This applied to the design of shops and offices as well as housing.

Developers respond to clear guidance

What was also notable was how quickly developers adapted to the situation once the guidance was definite and explicit. Conflicts between the planning committee and developers, described at the beginning of Chapter 5, occurred before this was the case. From 2001 onwards, there were almost no appeals against refusal of planning permission on design grounds. However, even with the very clear guidance, there was still an important role for negotiation. This went way beyond the processing of the formal planning applications. Two activities outside the formal process were critical for raising quality. Both pre-application negotiation and post-permission vigilance, and monitoring progress during detailed design and construction, paid dividends. When the process of effective design briefing and pre-application discussion was working properly, the processing of applications became largely a formality. Discussions started long before a planning application was submitted and the brief was written before the discussions started. They reflected a need to see how different sites fitted together and related to development over a larger area, even the town as a whole. This required considerable long-term vision regarding both the physical form and the formal process that brought it about.

Professional skills are needed

All these tasks depended on having professional officers with urban design skills operating above, and beyond, the development control process. What the Chelmsford's experience has shown is that appointing such people in sufficient numbers with the appropriate skills, and scope to carry out their job is the means to success. There was recognition by councillors that sustainable growth went hand-in-hand with design, a commitment expressed by having a design champion at elected member level. They assembled a team of people with urban design skills and, importantly, a genuine dedication to the local area. This team put in place procedures for producing and approving planning guidance and embedding design in development control. Cross-service team-work with planning, highways, housing and parks professionals was established for major developments. Good working relationships with the major developers were built up so they knew how the council operated and felt able to have a dialogue at any time. Professional officers nurtured a culture of wanting to improve development, to get the best out of sites, to insist on good designers and to have confidence in design.

Aside from new appointments, what also proved important was the influence that a leading councillor and chief officer could bring to bear in changing mind-sets of existing staff, changing the emphasis of planning from legalistic to spatial. This showed that even local planning authorities without urban design specialists should still be able to nurture an ethos of understanding site and context, of defining design objectives and issues, and establishing the discipline of scrutiny and challenge.

All need to work together

Although attention to organisational structure was important, it was not so much the precise structure that was adopted (the council's corporate structure changed several times) but the organisational culture. What was created was not a 'design section' but a team of urban designers who were integrated into the planning authority's overall task of managing development. Although the scale of the challenge should not be underestimated, the pursuit of team-work, rather than just consultation, was very significant. The different sections of a planning office needed to work closely together and to work closely with engineers, housing, parks and legal officers as required, all concentrating on getting the best quality of development rather than pursuing sectional interests. Changing departmental boundaries alone did not bring this about. The process of writing of the planning briefs and other policy documents proved to be a means of bringing people together at an early stage.

Positive negotiation gets results

The experience at Chelmsford showed that planning authorities could change developer practices. Chelmsford got house builders to appoint good architects, to modify or drop standard house-types and to design new house-types and one-off buildings. Through negotiation the planning authority:

- achieved neighbourhoods designed around public spaces, with continuous frontage, buildings turning corners and hiding car parking;
- negotiated well-integrated affordable housing and non-residential uses in high-density schemes;
- ensured development was based on legible routes and meaningful spaces to generate a sense of place;
- treated highway design as part of the landscape architecture and, where appropriate, tried to 'lose the road' in good shared surfaces;
- adopted the procedures for integrating usable green spaces into new places;
- used the quality of the public realm to glue the whole place together.

A last word

This book has advocated a proactive attitude to urban design. This means being evangelical about design, seeing opportunities, visualising outcomes and communicating design objectives. It means being positive about development, being constructively critical and taking risks to prompt innovation. It is not necessary to be an urban designer to such an attitude, but it opens up the way to design-led development and away from schemes led by standards, precedent, expediency, car parking or engineering.

The real process is understanding the nature of the place, generating a vision for the future, knowing what its citizens want and need, shaping new communities and steering implementation. This ought to be an exciting task for a council. It is positive planning. Rather than being seen merely as regulatory constraint, it ought to be viewed as a means of allowing design to reveal possibilities. The planning process is, in reality, one of analysis, problem solving, collaboration, enabling and explaining decisions.

In short, quality achievement on the ground has come from having vision, making their implications of this vision very clear in advance to all parties and providing the expertise to carry it though. The ultimate test is how this physical form stands the test of time. Readers are encouraged to visit the town and make their own judgement, hopefully using this book as a guide. What they should find is that the life of the town now speaks for itself.

References

Bentley, Ian, Alcock, Alan, Murrain, Paul, McGlynn, Sue and Smith, Graham (1985) *Responsive Environments: A Manual for Designers*, London: Architectural Press.

Billingham, John and Cole, Richard (2002) *The Good Place Guide*, London: Batsford.

CABE (2004) *Housing Audit: Assessing the Quality of New Homes*, London: Commission for Architecture and the Built Environment.

CABE (2006) *Design at Appeal,* London: Commission for Architecture and the Built Environment.

CABE and ODPM (2002*) Paving the Way*, London: Thomas Telford.

CBC (1994) *Springfield Basin and Chelmer Waterside*, Chelmsford, Essex: Chelmsford Borough Council.

CBC (1995) *Chelmsford Borough Local Plan Deposit Draft Inspector's Report*, Chelmsford, Essex: Chelmsford Borough Council.

CBC (1996a) *Land Off Princes Road,* Chelmsford, Essex: Chelmsford Borough Council.

CBC (1996b) *Land North East of Chelmsford*, Chelmsford, Essex: Chelmsford Borough Council.

CBC (1996c) *Land West of Main Road, Great Leighs*, Chelmsford, Essex: Chelmsford Borough Council.

CBC (1997a) *Chelmsford Borough Local Plan*, Chelmsford, Essex: Chelmsford Borough Council.

CBC (1997b) *Land East of Chelmer Village Way, Chelmsford*, Chelmsford, Essex: Chelmsford Borough Council.

CBC (1999a) *Former Marconi College, Arbour Lane, Chelmsford*, Chelmsford, Essex: Chelmsford Borough Council.

CBC (1999b) *Chelmer Waterside Area 1: Former Gas Works and Adjoining Land*, Chelmsford, Essex: Chelmsford Borough Council.

CBC (2000a) *West End Master Plan*, Chelmsford, Essex: Chelmsford Borough Council.

CBC (2000b) *Bus Station and Depot, Fairfield Road, Chelmsford*, Chelmsford, Essex: Chelmsford Borough Council.

CBC (2000c) *Village Design Statements – Advice on the Adoption of Village Design Statements as Supplementary Planning Guidance*, Chelmsford, Essex: Chelmsford Borough Council.

CBC (2001a) *Chelmsford Borough Local Plan Deposit Draft*, Chelmsford, Essex: Chelmsford Borough Council.

CBC (2001b) *Great Leighs Master Plan*, Chelmsford, Essex: Chelmsford Borough Council.

CBC (2001c) *Beaulieu Park Northern Area*, Chelmsford, Essex: Chelmsford Borough Council.

CBC (2001d) *Anglia Polytechnic University Central Campus and Adjoining Land, Victoria Road South, Chelmsford*, Chelmsford, Essex: Chelmsford Borough Council.

CBC (2002a) *Land East of High Street, Chelmsford*, Chelmsford, Essex: Chelmsford Borough Council.

CBC (2002b) *Land at Baddow Road and Beehive Lane, Chelmsford*, Chelmsford, Essex: Chelmsford Borough Council.

CBC (2002c) *Chelmer Waterside Strategy*, Chelmsford, Essex: Chelmsford Borough Council.

CBC (2002d) *Chelmer Waterside Area 4: Land North East of Canal*, Chelmsford, Essex: Chelmsford Borough Council.

CBC (2002e) *Drivers Yard and Mail Sorting Office, Victoria Road*, Chelmsford, Essex: Chelmsford Borough Council.

CBC (2003a) *Council Depot and Garage Court Site, between Meadgate Avenue and Baddow Road, Great Baddow*, Chelmsford, Essex: Chelmsford Borough Council.

CBC (2003b) *Car Dealership Site, 112 Parkway, Chelmsford*, Chelmsford, Essex: Chelmsford Borough Council.

CBC (2003c) *St. John's Hospital (former Chelmsford Union Workhouse), Wood Street, Chelmsford*, Chelmsford, Essex: Chelmsford Borough Council.

CBC (2003d) *BAe Systems Car Park, West Hanningfield Road, Great Baddow*, Chelmsford, Essex: Chelmsford Borough Council.

CBC (2005a) *Section 106 Agreements – Planning Guidance*, Chelmsford, Essex: Chelmsford Borough Council.

CBC (2005b) *Submitting Clear Plans & Information: A Guide for Developers*, Chelmsford, Essex: Chelmsford Borough Council.

CBC (2005c) *How to Do a Site and Context Analysis: A Guide for Developers*, Chelmsford, Essex: Chelmsford Borough Council.

CBC (2006) *St. John's Hospital, Wood Street, Chelmsford*, Chelmsford, Essex: Chelmsford Borough Council.

CBC and Great Waltham PC (2002) *Great Waltham Village Design Statement*, Chelmsford, Essex: Chelmsford Borough Council.

Countryside Commission (1993) *Design in the Countryside*, Technical Paper CCP418 Cheltenham: Countryside Commission.

Countryside Commission (1994) *Design in the Countryside Experiments*, Technical Paper CCP473 (prepared by BDOR Ltd.) Cheltenham: Countryside Commission.

DETR (1998a) *Planning for Sustainable Development: Towards Better Practice*, London: DETR.

DETR (1998b) *Places, Streets and Movement*, London: DETR.

DETR (2000a) *PPG3 Housing*, London: HMSO.

DETR (2000b) *Our Towns and Cities: The Future – Delivering an Urban Renaissance*, London: HMSO.

DETR and CABE (2000) *By Design*, London: DETR.

DoE and DTp (1977) *Design Bulletin 32, Residential Roads and Footpaths: Layout Considerations*, first edition, London: HMSO.

DoE and DTp (1992) *Design Bulletin 32, Residential Roads and Footpaths: Layout Considerations*, second edition, London: HMSO.

DTLR and CABE (2001) *By Design – Better Places to Live*, London: Thomas Telford.

ECC (1973) *A Design Guide for Residential Areas*, Chelmsford: Essex County Council.

ECC (1980) *A Design Guide for Residential Areas: Highway Standards* Chelmsford: Essex County Council.

ECC (1991) *Essex Structure Plan First Alteration*, Chelmsford: Essex County Council.

ECC (1995) *Essex Structure Plan Second Alteration*, Chelmsford: Essex County Council.

EPOA (1997) *A Design Guide for Residential and Mixed Use Areas*, Chelmsford: Essex County Council.

Hall, Anthony C. (1996) *Design Control: Towards a New Approach*, Oxford: Butterworth-Heinemann

Hall, Tony and Estop, Roger (2004) Chelmsford's Pro-active Approach to Making Better Places, *Planning*, 19th March, p. 22.

Hall, Tony (2006) A Plea for Front Gardens, *Urban Design*, 97, pp. 14–16.

Hardy, Dennis (2006) *Poundbury, The Town That Charles Built,* London: TCPA.

Llewelyn Davies, English Partnerships and the Housing Corporation (2000) *Urban Design Compendium,* London: English Partnerships and the Housing Corporation.

MfE (2005) *Urban Design Protocol,* Auckland: Ministry for the Environment.

MoT (1963) *Traffic in Towns,* London: HMSO.

UTF (1999) *Towards an Urban Renaissance,* London: Spon.

Index

Note: Page numbers in *italics* denote boxes, figures and tables